AN
INTENSE MOMENT
IN JERUSALEM

SCRIPTURE

Every year his parents went to Jerusalem for the Feast of the Passover. When he was twelve years old, they went up to the Feast, according to the custom. After the Feast was over, while his parents were returning home, the boy Jesus stayed behind in Jerusalem, but they were unaware of it. Thinking he was in their company, they traveled on for a day. Then they began looking for him among their relatives and friends. When they did not find him, they went back to Jerusalem to look for him. After three days they found him in the temple courts, sitting among the teachers, listening to them and asking them questions. Everyone who heard him was amazed at his understanding and his answers. When his parents saw him, they were astonished. His mother said to him, "Son, why have you treated us like this? Your father and I have been anxiously searching for you."

"Why were you searching for me?" he asked. "Didn't you know I had to be in my Father's house?" But they did not understand what he was saying to them.

Then he went down to Nazareth with them and was obedient to them. But his mother treasured all these things in her heart. And Jesus grew in wisdom and stature, and in favor with God and men.

Luke 2:41–52

MEDITATION

Jesus grew up full of boyish energy and boundless curiosity. Always asking his father about the meaning of Sabbath days and holy days. Always asking his mother to tell him the story of Samson or the Exodus one more time before snuffing out the oil lamp that allowed shadows to play on his bedroom wall.

But as Jesus grew up, so did his questions. His attention turned from the miracles in Exodus to the sacrifices in Leviticus. From stories about Samson in Judges to stories about the suffering servant in Isaiah.

He asked questions you would have never expected from a little boy. But then, Jesus wasn't a little boy anymore.

He was twelve now and had left his mother's side to take the side of his father. There he apprenticed in the family business, learning the care of tools and how to use them, the character of woods and how to shape them, the cost of materials and how to price them.

Jesus was no longer Mary's little boy. He had stepped across the threshold that separated his childhood from his adulthood. He was *Bar Mitzvah*, a "son of the Law." His training would be more formal now, with teachers and tutors and annual trips to the temple.

One of those trips was to celebrate Passover. The pilgrimage from Nazareth to Jerusalem wound eighty miles through hill country. Their caravan was a loose string of camels and donkeys, tied together by knots of women in front and men in back, and braided with strands of children that wove back and forth between the two. The children skipped and played games to pass the time, throwing rocks down ravines and cupping their ears to catch the echoes.

As they crested the final hill, the children gasped at the panorama of the holy city. Jesus' eyes passed over Herod's palace, with its stately columns and steps of marble, and rested on the temple. The expansive structure dazzled in the sun like a nugget of gold embedded in rock.

Together the men sang one of the Psalms of Ascent, a collection of psalms traditionally sung by pilgrims on their way to the holy city:

> Those who trust in the Lord are like Mount Zion,
> which cannot be shaken but endures forever.
> As the mountains surround Jerusalem,
> so the Lord surrounds his people
> both now and forevermore.

Jesus' heart raced as he joined in. The closer they got to the city, the louder they sang, and the more the young boy's heart pounded.

During Passover the city's population swelled to over two million people. Streets were clotted with pilgrims, days of sweat reeking from their garments, miles of dust caked on their skin, and the smell of their animals following them around like wet puppies.

But smells were a part of the holiday. The smell of herbs being crushed into paste. The smell of lambs roasting over open pits. The smell of unleavened bread baking in stone ovens. As much as anything, smells brought back the memory of the first Passover.

The bitter herbs recalled the nation's enslavement to Egypt. The roasting lamb recalled the night each Jewish household sacrificed a lamb and sprinkled its blood on their doorposts so the angel of death would pass over their home. The unleavened bread recalled their hurried departure, that allowed them no time to wait for yeast to rise.

And so the smells were nostalgic. Especially the smell of lamb. For more than any others, it was savory with the aroma of salvation.

Joseph takes Jesus by the hand into the outer courtyard, looking for a lamb for the family's meal. The young boy gapes at the immense pillars, the columns surrounding them like a regiment of stone soldiers. His hand slips from his father's as he turns to take it all in.

All around him is the sound of buying and selling. The complaining about prices. The clinking of silver. The exchanging of merchandise. Everything from souvenirs to sacrificial animals is for sale. Doves in wooden cages. Calves on tethers. Lambs crowded into makeshift pens. The bleating of beasts rises like a dirge.

Jesus watches his father inspect a skittish huddle of lambs. According to the Law, the sacrifice has to be male, without spot or blemish or broken bone. Joseph singles one out and gathers the nervous wool into his arms. He drapes the lamb over his shoulders, and they enter the inner courtyard.

The mood is reverential, somber and subdued. In the middle of the courtyard, a large altar sends the smoke of sacrifices curling into the sky. Joseph gives the lamb to a priest, who draws his knife and pulls back the lamb's head.

Jesus winces but does not look away.

With a quick slash, the body goes limp. The woolen neck turns soppy with blood, which is caught in a vessel and poured around the altar. Another slash of the knife, and the entrails spill out. Jesus winces again. The priest makes a few more cuts and heaps the organs onto the altar. He hands the carcass back to Joseph.

Joseph takes it away and trusses it up, stretching out its limbs. He works his knife steadily and methodically, as he separates the skin from its body. He drives a wooden skewer vertically through the breast, then one horizontally through the forelegs, to make roasting it easier.

Stained with blood, the wood resembles the doorposts that were passed over in ancient Egypt.

After Passover, they stay a week longer to celebrate the Feast of Unleavened Bread. It is a good week but a long time to be away, and so the caravan packs up and heads home.

The women start out together, the men bring up the rear, and the children are everywhere in between. They start early in the morning and stop late in the afternoon. As families reunite to pitch their tents, Mary asks Joseph about Jesus.

"I thought he was with you," he answers.

Mary's face goes suddenly slack.

"He's probably just with the other boys," he says, trying to calm her.

But they look, and he is not with the other boys. They go to their relatives. But he is not with the relatives. They question their friends. But he is not with them either.

Now Joseph becomes concerned, too, and they take the fastest donkeys back to Jerusalem. A sharp pain causes Mary to reach for her side. Is it the jostling of the donkey? Is it anxiety? Or is it the tip of the sword Simeon prophesied?

She knows a sword lies in her future. *Will it come tonight, on this road?* she asks herself. *Or tomorrow, in Jerusalem?*

She prays. *Please protect him, Lord. He may be a man in the eyes of the Law, but he's still a little boy to me.*

They ride all night, stopping at encampments along the way, asking strangers if they have seen a twelve-year-old, so tall and named Jesus. The limestone cliffs gleam in the moonlight and give enough light for them to look down the ravines on the side of the road for any traces of a body.

Joseph tries to allay her fears, telling her all the places Jesus might be and how safe it is in the holy city, especially this time of the year. But Mary knows Jerusalem. It has its back alleys and bad neighborhoods, just like any big city. And there are beggars and transients and the riffraff of the Roman army.

Once inside the city, they retrace their every step. They

accost strangers in the street. "Have you seen our son? He's twelve. Just a boy."

They knock on neighborhood doors. "We're looking for a boy from Nazareth. His name is Jesus. Have you seen him?"

They talk with merchants. But no one has seen him.

For three days they search. And for three days they don't know if he's lost and looking for them, or lying in some back alley. They don't know if he's been kidnapped or killed. For three intense days they scour the streets, not knowing if they will ever see their son again.

Finally, they go to the temple. They go, not to search but to pray.

When they enter the courtyard, they see an inquisitive circle of teachers. In the midst of them is . . .

Jesus!

Mary runs to him, a rush of relief and anger welling up within her. "Son, why have you treated us like this? Your father and I have been anxiously searching for you."

Jesus looks at her in a way he's never looked at her before. "Why were you searching for me? Didn't you know I had to be in my Father's house?"

Mary looks to Joseph, but a shrug of the shoulders is all the explanation he can give. As they leave the temple, Mary collects herself. Her little boy is safe, and that's all that matters.

Once again this child has unsettled her life.

So much mystery surrounds him. She knows the mystery has something to do with saving the world from its sin, but she doesn't know how. She suspects it has something to do with Passover, but she doesn't know what. She fears it has something to do with suffering, but she doesn't know why.

This much she does know:

There is no fear like the fear of losing a child.

She felt that fear the night they fled to Egypt. She felt it again these past three days. And she knows she will feel it every time he's late for dinner. Every time he runs a fever. Every time he sleeps too soundly or too long.

Though she was learning to let go, there would always be a part of her that would be holding on to his hand. And for this mother—who gave him life, who nursed him and bathed him, who told him stories and sang him to sleep—there would always be a part of him that would remain . . . her little boy.

PRAYER

ear Lord,

Thank you for Mary. She loved you the way only a mother could. She knew you the way no other person on earth could know you. She saw your first smile, heard your first word, helped you take your first step.

Thank you for all the time she spent holding you, cuddling you, telling you stories. Thank you for everything she did to help you grow in wisdom and stature, and in favor with God and men.

Thank you for her maternal instincts that protected you during your formative years. Thank you for her obedience in fleeing to Egypt to save you, and for her diligence in searching through Jerusalem to find you.

I know if I love you the way she loved you, my heart will never be safe. Someday you will unsettle my life. And someday a sword will pierce my heart too.

Prepare me for that day, Lord. Help me to realize that the greater my love for you, the sharper that sword will be . . . and the deeper it will go.

Help me to understand that risk.

And help me to understand, as I try to fathom the mystery of your love for me, that it's the one risk in this world really worth taking. . . .

AN
INTENSE MOMENT
AT THE
JORDAN RIVER

SCRIPTURE

In those days John the Baptist came, preaching in the Desert of Judea and saying, "Repent, for the kingdom of heaven is near." This is he who was spoken of through the prophet Isaiah:

"A voice of one calling in the desert,
'Prepare the way for the Lord,
    make straight paths for him.'"

John's clothes were made of camel's hair, and he had a leather belt around his waist. His food was locusts and wild honey. People went out to him from Jerusalem and all Judea and the whole region of the Jordan. Confessing their sins, they were baptized by him in the Jordan River.

But when he saw many of the Pharisees and Sadducees coming to where he was baptizing, he said to them: "You brood of vipers! Who warned you to flee from the coming wrath? Produce fruit in keeping with repentance. And do not think you can say to yourselves, 'We have Abraham as our father.' I tell you that out of these stones God can raise up children for Abraham. The ax is already at the root of the trees, and every tree that does not produce good fruit will be cut down and thrown into the fire.

"I baptize you with water for repentance. But after me will come one who is more powerful than I, whose sandals I am not fit to carry. He will baptize you with the Holy Spirit and with fire. His winnowing fork is in his hand, and he will clear his threshing floor, gathering his wheat into the barn and burning up the chaff with unquenchable fire."

Then Jesus came from Galilee to the Jordan to be baptized by John. But John tried to deter him, saying, "I need to be baptized by you, and do you come to me?"

Jesus replied, "Let it be so now; it is proper for us to do this to fulfill all righteousness." Then John consented.

As soon as Jesus was baptized, he went up out of the water. At that moment heaven was opened, and he saw the Spirit of God descending like a dove and lighting on him. And a voice from heaven said, "This is my Son, whom I love; with him I am well pleased."

Matthew 3

MEDITATION

Years have passed since Jesus' boyhood. And so much more has passed besides the years. In Rome, Caesar Augustus' throne has passed to Tiberius. In Nazareth, Joseph's carpentry shop has passed to Jesus.

And now, something else is passing.

At the end of the day Jesus sweeps up the wood shavings on the floor of the shop for the last time. He stands the broom by the doorway and looks back. The fresh-cut smell of sawdust is fragrant with memories.

Memories of Joseph wrapping his large hands around the hands of an eager little boy as he showed him how to hold a saw, pound a hammer, plane a piece of wood. Memories of the carts they made, the furniture, the tools. Memories of the lunches they shared, the conversations, the laughter.

As he closes the door, Jesus says goodbye to those memories. But before he leaves his life as a carpenter, there is one more goodbye he has to say.

It is a goodbye his mother knew was coming. But knowing didn't make it any easier.

We have no record of what Jesus said to her. Or what she said to him. And maybe that is good. Goodbyes are so private and personal, so filled with tears and tender gestures. The stroke of a cheek. The squeeze of a hand. The hug. The kiss. The last, rending goodbye.

After Jesus hugs her and kisses her and says goodbye,

he turns and walks away. Mary goes inside and slumps in a chair. Everything she has treasured in her heart for so many years pushes its way to the surface and comes spilling down her cheeks.

While she sits at home, alone with her thoughts, Jesus walks some fifteen miles eastward until he comes to the rim of the Jordan Valley. The valley is an unsightly scar on the landscape that stretches between the Sea of Galilee and the Dead Sea. The Jordan River brings life to the thirsty valley. Its tufted banks are fringed with green, with reeds and tamarisks and bent-over willows that drop their leaves into the water like tears.

All sorts of people are gathered there. Merchants. Soldiers. Tax collectors. Religious leaders. Ordinary, everyday people. Or so it looks on the outside.

On the inside, things look different. On the inside there are lies and deceit and fraud; there are idolatries and adulteries; there are hateful words and vengeful reprisals; there are thefts and murders and a litany of broken laws, broken vows, broken relationships.

Into this valley of brokenness Jesus now descends to where the Jordan flows three hundred feet below sea level.

Waist deep in the sluggish water is a man known to the crowd only as John the Baptizer. But Jesus knows him as the son of a relative on his mother's side of the family. Elizabeth's boy. Except he's not a boy anymore. How different he looks now. His face is maned with hair. His eyes are deep-set and intense. He gets his food by trapping locusts and digging into beehives with his bare hands. He looks like a camel when he kneels to drink from the Jordan, his body clad in a mangy tatter of skins that is cinched with a broad leather belt.

But his ragged exterior hides his inner strength, for his words are like lightning and his voice like thunder. At times you thought it would split the very rocks around you. His aim, though, was not to split rocks but hearts.

"Repent!" he calls out, and hearts crumble. You can hear the brokenness all along the banks. And with the word "repent," you realize the obstacles in the way to their returning to God are not intellectual but moral. They are the gullies of eroded character and the gaping potholes left by the washout of sin.

One by one the people come forward. And out of the gravel of their broken hearts, John begins to pave a highway in the desert—a highway for the coming King.

But when that King comes, he comes to be baptized. Along with all the others. John can't believe it. For what did Jesus need to repent?

For nothing.

That is both the mystery and the majesty of his baptism.

Witness the humiliation of God.

At his birth, he stepped from heaven to take on our flesh. At his baptism, he steps down even further to take on our shame. He descends into the valley of repentance, willing not only to stand on the banks with us in our humanness but also to wade in the water to stand with us in our sinfulness.

How far would the Savior go? To what depths would he descend in wooing an indifferent world?

From the heavens descends the soft flutter of God's Spirit. As it settles on Jesus' shoulders, the people stare and wonder. Who is this for whom heaven opens and upon whom the Spirit of God settles so tamely?

A voice from heaven thunders the answer:

"This is my Son, whom I love; with him I am well pleased."

But what has this Son accomplished to merit such approval?

He hasn't taught in the synagogue or triumphed over Satan. He hasn't preached a sermon or cast out a demon. He hasn't healed a sick person or made a single disciple. He hasn't done anything special, let alone spectacular.

So why was his Father so pleased?

Maybe it was the same pleasure Joseph had when he saw the young Jesus standing next to him in the shop, miming his every move as he worked the wood with his hands. Though the boy had not made anything of his own, he was so eager to learn and so willing to work. He was so attentive to his father's voice and so submissive to his instructions. He went about his apprenticeship with such joy, humming his way through the day. For he delighted in working with his father. Even if he was given the lowliest of work to do. Regardless of whether it was stooping to pick up scraps of wood or sweeping the sawdust off the floor.

Jesus' baptism marked his passage into a new apprenticeship. The apprenticeship of suffering. It would be the hardest work he would ever do. And the lowliest.

But he would be working with his Father, listening to his every word, following his every instruction. And he would be working with delight.

What father wouldn't be pleased with a son like that?

PRAYER

earest Jesus,

Thank you for being such a good Son. For your eagerness to learn from your Father. For your willingness to do his work. For your attentiveness to his voice and your obedience to his will.

While you were on earth, you said you could do nothing on your own but only what you saw the Father doing, and could speak nothing on your own but only what the Father had taught you.

Your dream in life was to fulfill his. To see his dream for the world come true. To see his dream for individuals come true. Help me to see people like that, Lord. To see what they could be if his dream for their life was fulfilled. And then grant me the grace, I pray, so my words and actions might serve to help that dream come true.

Help me to realize that many of those dreams would never come true apart from suffering. And that even though you were a beloved Son, you learned obedience from the things you suffered. If that was true for you, how much more must it be true for me.

Give me such a oneness with the Father that his dreams would be my dreams. That his will would be my will. That his words would be my words. And that the driving ambition in my life would be to please him.

Lord, the last words you spoke to your disciples were about your Father. In that upper room you said you would continue to work so that the love the Father has for you would be in them and in us.

Could that be true? Is it possible I could love you the way the Father loves you? Even remotely possible? Could I delight in you the way he delights in you? Could you be the passion of my life the way you are his?

If so, Lord Jesus, I pray you would give me that love, that delight, that passion.

I know the Father loves me simply because I am his child. I only hope that someday, when he looks down from heaven at my life, he will be well pleased with this child.

And I know if I spend the rest of my life loving you the way he does, he will be. . . .

An
INTENSE MOMENT
IN THE
DESERT

SCRIPTURE

Then Jesus was led by the Spirit into the desert to be tempted by the devil. After fasting forty days and forty nights, he was hungry. The tempter came to him and said, "If you are the Son of God, tell these stones to become bread."

Jesus answered, "It is written: 'Man does not live on bread alone, but on every word that comes from the mouth of God.'"

Then the devil took him to the holy city and had him stand on the highest point of the temple. "If you are the Son of God," he said, "throw yourself down. For it is written:

"'He will command his angels concerning you,
and they will lift you up in their hands,
so that you will not strike your foot against a stone.'"

Jesus answered him, "It is also written: 'Do not put the Lord your God to the test.'"

Again, the devil took him to a very high mountain and showed him all the kingdoms of the world and their splendor. "All this I will give you," he said, "if you will bow down and worship me."

Jesus said to him, "Away from me, Satan! For it is written: 'Worship the Lord your God, and serve him only.'"

Then the devil left him, and angels came and attended him.

Matthew 4:1–11

MEDITATION

he desert is where we face the strongest and most seductive temptations in life. It is where the enemy is most formidable and where we are most vulnerable.

Into such a desert Jesus is now led.

It stretches before him like an endless wasteland, frayed with gullies, littered with splintered rock and sun-bleached bones. Stoop-shouldered hills are hunched all around him. At his feet, impoverished plants reach skyward, like beggars desperate for alms. But the eyes of heaven are unsympathetic. They offer no tears. Only the compensatory promise of night.

As the sun goes down, the earth relinquishes its heat like a sigh. Great shafts of light alternate with shadow, and the horizon becomes a grim silhouette.

As Jesus searches for a place to sleep, his Father's last words accompany him. So do the last words of John.

"Look, the Lamb of God—"

Jesus knows what those words mean. He had been to the temple. He had seen the altar.

"—who takes away the sin of the world!"

He remembers the smoke from that altar, wisping toward heaven like a prayer. He remembers the priest. And the knife. And the blood.

For forty days and forty nights he remembers.

It is his last day in the desert, and the muted grandeur of dusk turns to halftones, rendering the hills flat and featureless. Shadows seek refuge in alcoves of overhanging rock, as if trying to muster courage to step into the receding light. One by one they creep from behind boulders and steal past chalky outcroppings of rock.

The moon rises from the horizon and softens the edges of the mountains. Limestone escarpments gleam like icebergs in some dark, far-off sea. In the moon-washed night, the desert comes alive. Crawling insects emerge from their holes. Cautious rodents scurry over sand. Cold-blooded reptiles slither over rocks.

Jesus settles in a shallow cave scalloped out of the hillside. His only bed is the cold hard ground; his only blanket, the dark of night.

Mark tells us that while Jesus was in the desert he was "among the wild animals." Like some distant scent, a memory of paradise drifts past those animals and starts them salivating. They come forward, lean and haggard and hungry. Timidly at first. Sniffing him out.

Their presence is a collective prayer. A prayer for that place where the wolf and the lamb could lie down together. A prayer for the return of Eden.

They sense this man is the answer to that prayer. And at the mouth of that cave, almost as if guarding the entrance to paradise, they lie down together and sleep.

The next morning the stretching sun flings great handfuls of color onto the gray landscape. It is barely up and already its anger can be felt, growing hot and white in its ascent.

Jesus wakes and pushes his weakened frame from the cool dirt. His angular features look as if they have been chiseled from a slab of rock. His skin is parched. His lips are cracked. And, after forty days of fasting, he is famished.

A strategic time to strike, thinks Satan, as he steps from the shadows. His movements are wary, for he is unsure whether he will end up as predator or prey. He takes a tentative step forward and grows bold in seeing how thin and frail his opponent has become.

"If you are the Son of God, tell these stones to become bread."

The temptation is not to make Jesus doubt himself but to depend on himself. Since the Father hasn't lifted a finger to alleviate his suffering, why not take things into his own hands? After all, it's been forty days. Who would blame him?

But Jesus doesn't take the baited hook. Instead he answers, "It is written: 'Man does not live on bread alone, but on every word that comes from the mouth of God.'"

Regardless how consuming his hunger, Jesus would rather be fed with the smallest crust of his Father's word than with an entire landscape of fresh bread from anywhere else.

Satan steps back to plan his next move. A change of strategy might help. And a change of scenery. He brings Jesus to the pinnacle of the temple and prods him with the blunt end of the very weapon Jesus used against him.

"If you are the Son of God," he said, "throw yourself down. For it is written: 'He will command his angels concerning you, and they will lift you up in their hands, so that you will not strike your foot against a stone.'"

In the first temptation Jesus answered Satan by affirming his dependence on the Father, so in this temptation Satan pushes that dependence to the limit. *If you really believe God will take care of you*, reasons Satan, *let him prove it, and prove it publicly, so everyone can see.*

The temple was the center of religious activity for Israel. The jump would be seen by all the key leaders. And the rescue would convince them that Jesus was indeed the Son of God. In a single act he could win over every skeptic and avoid years of conflict with the religious establishment.

A tempting offer.

But Jesus sees through it, realizing that such a test would not be a confirmation of God's care but a calling of his care into question. Without hesitating, he replies:

"It is also written: 'Do not put the Lord your God to the test.'"

Such a test would say to God: "If you really care about me, prove it." The challenge does not demonstrate faith in God's care; it demonstrates a doubt that needs some tangible proof before we will be convinced.

Rebuffed, Satan steps back and regroups. He then takes Jesus to an even greater pinnacle, for an even greater temptation. As god of this world, Satan has the earthly kingdoms in his pocket. He digs into that pocket and counts the change. He makes a final offer.

"All this I will give you," he said, "if you will bow down and worship me."

These are the kingdoms the Father has promised Jesus. These are the kingdoms he would someday possess. That someday could be today. And all of tomorrow's suffering could be avoided. All he would have to do is turn his back for a moment and merely bend a knee in Satan's direction. That's all.

But it is *who* he would have to turn his back on that keeps his knees locked. His own Father. His Father who loves him and delights in him. How could he bend even a knee, even for a moment, in betrayal of such a relationship?

Jesus takes the loose change and throws it in Satan's face.

"Away from me, Satan! For it is written: 'Worship the Lord your God, and serve him only.'"

The words snap like a whip. Satan recoils, his lip wrinkled in derision, and turns to leave. He leaves, Luke tells us, until a more "opportune time," a time when Jesus would be weaker, more vulnerable, a time when his suffering would be more intense—a time he could have avoided, if only he hadn't taken sides in that desert so decisively, and resisted so resolutely.

In the Jordan, Jesus was anointed by the Holy Spirit and approved by the Father. In the desert, he appeared abandoned by both. Every trace of God was swept away by the wind or buried by the sand. There was no affirming voice. There was no attesting sign.

All Jesus heard from heaven was the hollow whistling of the wind. All he saw when he looked up were vultures circling in ever-narrowing patterns.

Yet still he trusted.

Still he obeyed.

And only afterward did angels come.

PRAYER

 ear Lord,

Help me to trust you at all times, but especially in the desert experiences of my life. When I am tempted to live by sight rather than by faith. When I am tempted to depend on myself rather than you. When I am tempted to question your love. And when I am tempted to defect.

Give me the faith, I pray, that Habakkuk had in his desert experience:

> Though the fig tree does not bud
> and there are no grapes on the vines,
> though the olive crop fails
> and the fields produce no food,
> though there are no sheep in the pen
> and no cattle in the stalls,
> yet I will rejoice in the Lord,
> I will be joyful in God my Savior.
>
> The Sovereign Lord is my strength;
> he makes my feet like the feet of a deer,
> he enables me to go on the heights.

Help me to see that the Father's word is not only more nourishing than food but more necessary. And that he decrees bread or stones according to which one at the moment provides the best nourishment for my soul.

Help me never to doubt your love for me, Lord. And keep me from the temptation of ever putting that love to the test. Keep me from being enticed by whatever trinkets

Satan dangles before me. And guard me from the temptation of wanting anything more than I want you.

Give me the thirst to study God's word as you studied
it. But help me realize that it was not knowledge of his
word that delivered you—even Satan had that—but it was
your obedience to his word that brought you safely through
temptation.

Lead me not into temptation, Lord, but deliver me from
the Evil One. You know how weak I am and how vulnerable to his deceptions. But should you ever lead me into
some desert to be tempted by him, help me to realize that
greater is he that is in me than he that is in the world. And
that if I resist Satan, he will flee.

Thank you that you have been tempted in every way
that I am tempted, and are sympathetic to my struggles.
Thank you that I can come boldly to your throne of grace
and there not only find mercy but understanding. . . .

AN INTENSE MOMENT AT THE TEMPLE

SCRIPTURE

When it was almost time for the Jewish Passover, Jesus went up to Jerusalem. In the temple courts he found men selling cattle, sheep and doves, and others sitting at tables exchanging money. So he made a whip out of cords, and drove all from the temple area, both sheep and cattle; he scattered the coins of the money changers and overturned their tables. To those who sold doves he said, "Get these out of here! How dare you turn my Father's house into a market!"

His disciples remembered that it is written: "Zeal for your house will consume me."

Then the Jews demanded of him, "What miraculous sign can you show us to prove your authority to do all this?"

Jesus answered them, "Destroy this temple, and I will raise it again in three days."

The Jews replied, "It has taken forty-six years to build this temple, and you are going to raise it in three days?" But the temple he had spoken of was his body.

John 2:13–21

MEDITATION

very Passover, every Jewish house went through a ceremonial spring cleaning. Cupboards were scrubbed to the corners and walls to the ceilings. Floors were swept and reswept.

But all the sweeping and scrubbing wasn't to get rid of dirt. It was to get rid of yeast. For during Passover, possession of even the smallest amount was forbidden. The Law was specific, and the penalty strict.

So the removal of yeast was serious business. It was also a serious reminder. Reminding every Jewish family of the Exodus. Of the hurried departure in the middle of the night. Of the rushing to bake bread for the journey. And since there was no time to wait for dough to rise, yeast was removed from the recipe.

From that time on, removal of yeast became part of the Passover tradition. The night before the Passover meal the father would light a candle and lead the family in a final inspection. Every corner was examined. Every drawer. Every utensil. It was a solemn ceremony. Any yeast that was found or any food containing yeast was put in a designated place and destroyed.

So every Passover, every Jewish house was immaculate. Except one. In the hurry of preparing for the holiday, one house was overlooked.

The house of God.

Jesus has come to this house every Passover since he was twelve. And every year it seemed to get worse. The commercialism, that is. Every year more animals were sold, more money was exchanged, more booths were crowded into the courtyard.

Many of the booths were owned by the sons of Annas, the high priest. The residents of the holy city made a tidy profit at Passover, renting out rooms, providing services, selling sacrifices and souvenirs. Everyone did it. And so no one thought anything when the religious leaders did it too.

It was *where* they did it that made the offense so serious.

The buying and selling took place in the temple's outer courtyard. The inner courtyard was reserved for Jews, but the outer courtyard was set aside so Gentiles would have a place to come and pray. The very design of the temple reflected Israel's mission of outreach to the world, of gathering people from every tribe and nation within its gates, giving them access to God and an opportunity to become part of the community of faith.

But when Jesus enters this courtyard, he sees no light leading a lost world to God. The smothering commerce of the holiday has all but snuffed it out. His eyes peer through the stately colonnade. In the shadows he sees a Gentile off by himself, his eyes closed, his head bowed, his hands clasped in prayer.

From a nearby table a stack of coins tumbles to the floor, creating a scramble for loose change. A money changer pushes his way into the frenzy. One of the men he pushes stumbles into the Gentile, and his prayer is interrupted. The money changer dives to the ground, reaching between people's legs, rooting out his profit from underneath stubborn sandals.

Money changers served to keep the temple coffers unsoiled from foreign coinage. Every Jew had to pay the treasury an annual tax of half a shekel, but only specially minted coins were accepted for payment. Coins that were kosher. The exchange rate fluctuated with the character of each money changer. The lower the character, the higher the rate of exchange. And during Passover, rates were exorbitant.

Besides the clink of shekels, sounds of animals filled the courtyard, animals sold for sacrifices and for Passover meals. They were sold for many times what they were worth, but during the holiday it was a seller's market, and the animals that passed priestly inspection commanded a premium price.

With the animals came the smell of dung and urine. A wave of nausea washes over Jesus as he takes this all in. But it is not the stench of animals that sickens him. It is the stench of religion gone bad.

Making a profit at Passover had become central to the holiday. Not prayer. Not remembrance. Not thanksgiving. Maybe these things were central for the visiting pilgrim, but not for the vocational priest. The heart of the professional had long since lost its zeal for sacred things. His hands had long since grown calloused from the daily routine of religious responsibilities.

Jesus looks again at the Gentile who is trying to squeeze out a little solitude. But again his prayer is cut short, this time by someone brushing past him with a squirming lamb slung over his shoulder.

Jesus' nostrils flare. His jaws clench. Draped across a table is a handful of tethers. He snatches them up and ties them together. His face flushes. The veins in his neck protrude. His heart is a pounding fist. He pulls the knot tight.

When he cracks the whip a circle of men recoil, confusion mapped in every wrinkle and contour of their faces. Jesus kicks over a table, sending two of them tumbling backward, their money skipping along the marble floor. He pulls down a makeshift fence, and another smack of his whip sends a dozen lambs bleating for cover. He goes down the row, picking up the ends of tables and heaving them over.

He whirls his whip overhead, then strikes with a crack of leather. Men scatter like leaves before this whirlwind of a man as the wrath of heaven funnels down to earth, upending everything in its path.

Jesus storms through a tenement slum of bird cages with a hail of words for the man guarding them. "Get these out of here! How *dare* you turn my Father's house into a market!"

The anger is torrential, and it looks as if Jesus himself might be swept away. The disciples step back from the downpour. As they do, they remember the Scripture, which now appears prophetic:

"Zeal for your house will consume me."

They wonder. How long has it been since they've seen zeal like this? When was the last time they saw a priest seething at some injustice done to a widow or orphan? When was the last time they saw a Pharisee sobbing at his own sinfulness and pleading passionately to God for mercy? How long? They can't even remember. They wonder if they have ever seen it at all.

Until now.

But now, suddenly, they wonder something else.

They wonder what kind of boat they've gotten themselves into when they signed on as fishers of men. *What kind of strategy is this to launch a ministry? Doesn't Jesus realize the rift this will create with the religious leaders? Doesn't he know how many people he will alienate, how many enemies he will make?*

But another snap of his whip breaks up that crowd of thoughts. The bite of leather on the backs of merchants brings yelps of protest. But nobody stops him, nobody stands in his way.

Table by table, the religious flea market is overturned. People are slipping on fresh manure and sent sprawling, stumbling into each other and over animals. The wings of doves are flapping against the bars of their wicker prisons. The eyes of lambs are darting nervously for an opening in the stampede. The hooves of oxen are chattering over marble tiles in a frantic race for freedom.

Meanwhile, the more religious are standing back, cursing like Canaanites. And for good reason. Religion had become big business. The priests lived well. And they grew to love living well. They grew to love being surrounded by nice things, eating sumptuous meals, wearing fine clothes, receiving respectful greetings everywhere they went.

And they grew to love too the many perks of their profession—the table of honor at banquets, the generosity of benefactors, the elite social gatherings where they rubbed shoulders with politicians and well-connected people.

And maybe, in the end, that was their undoing.

For at some point the good life became more important than a good heart.

Which is why reaching into the pockets of the people became more important than reaching out to the world.

Which is how prayer got pushed out of the courtyard.

Which is why Jesus got so angry.

That Passover when Jesus came to the temple, he came to clean house. From the slender candle of his life flamed a zeal so intense it exposed the yeasty greed that was doughing up every corner of the courtyard.

His whip was merely the washrag that removed it.

Today zeal for his Father's house consumed him. One day it would kill him. Today the religious cursed him. One day they would crucify him.

All because he lit a candle . . .

and because of where he dared to shine it.

PRAYER

 hine, Jesus, shine.

Shine your light in every corner of my heart. Search every cupboard. Open every door to every closet. And bring whatever evil is hidden there out in the open.

Search me, O God, and know my heart. See if there is in me any small trace of hypocrisy, any small bit of impurity, any small beginnings of greed or materialism. Wash me, O Lord, and make me clean.

Forgive me for how I have overlooked the many small but pervasive influences that threatened to make a doughy mess of my life. For the small talk that grew into gossip. For the slight stretching of truth that grew into a lie. For the silent insecurities that grew into jealousies that grew into criticisms of others.

Forgive me for all I have tolerated in the courtyards of my life. For the way I have allowed sacred things to become profaned. For the way I have allowed prayer to be pushed to the far corners of my life.

Come, Lord Jesus. Come to the temple of my heart. Overturn the tables. Drive out the money changers. And do what you have to do to make it a place of prayer. . . .

AN
INTENSE MOMENT
ON A
MOUNTAIN

SCRIPTURE

From that time on Jesus began to explain to his disciples that he must go to Jerusalem and suffer many things at the hands of the elders, chief priests and teachers of the law, and that he must be killed and on the third day be raised to life.

Peter took him aside and began to rebuke him. "Never, Lord!" he said. "This shall never happen to you!"

Jesus turned and said to Peter, "Get behind me, Satan! You are a stumbling block to me; you do not have in mind the things of God, but the things of men."

Then Jesus said to his disciples, "If anyone would come after me, he must deny himself and take up his cross and follow me. For whoever wants to save his life will lose it, but whoever loses his life for me will find it. What good will it be for a man if he gains the whole world, yet forfeits his soul? Or what can a man give in exchange for his soul? For the Son of Man is going to come in his Father's glory with his angels, and then he will reward each person according to what he has done. I tell you the truth, some who are standing here will not taste death before they see the Son of Man coming in his kingdom."

After six days Jesus took with him Peter, James and John the brother of James, and led them up a high mountain by themselves. There he was transfigured before them. His face shone like the sun, and his clothes became as white as the light. Just then there appeared before them Moses and Elijah, talking with Jesus.

Peter said to Jesus, "Lord, it is good for us to be here. If you wish, I will put up three shelters—one for you, one for Moses and one for Elijah."

While he was still speaking, a bright cloud enveloped them, and a voice from the cloud said, "This is my Son, whom I love; with him I am well pleased. Listen to him!"

When the disciples heard this, they fell facedown to the ground, terrified. But Jesus came and touched them. "Get up," he said. "Don't be afraid." When they looked up, they saw no one except Jesus.

As they were coming down the mountain, Jesus instructed them, "Don't tell anyone what you have seen, until the Son of Man has been raised from the dead."

The disciples asked him, "Why then do the teachers of the law say that Elijah must come first?"

Jesus replied, "To be sure, Elijah comes and will restore all things. But I tell you, Elijah has already come, and they did not recognize him, but have done to him everything they wished. In the same way the Son of Man is going to suffer at their hands." Then the disciples understood that he was talking to them about John the Baptist.

Matthew 16:21–17:13

MEDITATION

Jesus announces that some who have heard him speak about his suffering won't die until they see him in his glory.

The "some" are Peter, James, and John.

They are the only three disciples Jesus took with him into the home of Jairus when he raised his daughter from the dead. And they will be the only three he takes with him into the heart of Gethsemane when he wrestles with his destiny.

He takes these three with him now up Mount Hermon. They pick their way through the pathless incline of weather-beaten rock. Up past the sweet-smelling grasses of the foothills. Up past the treeline. Up to a quiet place where they can stop and pray.

Once there, the footsore disciples bend over, their hands grabbing their knees, their lungs grabbing for air. They lean against sheer rock as rivulets of sweat run down their faces, sopped by the neckline of their garments. One by one they slump to the ground. As they catch their breath, their eyes slowly sweep the panorama.

The watercolors of late afternoon streak the sky, their dripping yellows gathering at the bottoms of clouds and tinting them orange. To the west lie the sun-kissed plains of the Promised Land. To the east, the blue slate of the Mediterranean. To the south, the watered lushness of the Jordan Valley.

They are halfway to heaven, or so it seems. Thousands

of feet above sea level, they are cut off from the world below. No teeming crowds. No torrents of controversy. Only clouds and sky and a soft stroke of wind brushing past their cheeks.

The climb up the mountain has been long and steep, and as Jesus goes off to pray, the disciples drift off to sleep. As he prays, a rush of adrenalin runs through him. Maybe it's from the climb. Or the claustrophobia.

His fate is closing in on him, and he feels as if the hounds of hell have been unleashed, have picked up his scent, and are baying in pursuit. The adrenalin pumping through his veins tells him to either fight or flee. But the adrenalin coursing through his spirit tells him to do neither. And so he calls to heaven for the strength to face the hounds, the strength to surrender, to give his neck to their ravenous jaws.

He prays for strength to descend the valley of suffering that awaits him. He prays for a ray of hope—however dim, however distant—to help him through the darkness of the days ahead.

Heaven answers, and the ray comes, awakening the disciples. They rub their squinting eyes. Standing before them is an incandescent silhouette, as if a blade of lightning had slashed the sky and let something of heaven spill through.

Blinding in its resplendence, the face of Jesus shines as the noonday sun. Seamless folds of light flow from his garments like so much fabric unfurling from a bolt of shimmering white cloth.

The bewildered disciples spring to their feet. Is this a dream? A vision? A hallucination brought on by the altitude and fatigue? They wonder these things as they shield their faces. Until the light grows more intense and hurts their eyes. They not only see the light, they feel it. Then they know. It is no dream. It is no vision. It is no hallucination.

Until now, the tent of Jesus' humanity has largely concealed his identity. But now the flap on that tent is lifted, and these privileged three are given a glimpse of his glory.

In the light of that glory all things around them have paled. The rocks and boulders, once bold and jutting, are now washed out of both color and character. The tufts of grass sprigging out from the rocks have lost their green. The dirt has surrendered its brown. There is no depth or dimension to anything around them. Everything has blanched and paled.

Now that they see the Savior in the glory he will have in his kingdom, there are no thoughts about who among them would be greatest in that kingdom. Those things have paled too.

As their eyes adjust they see Moses and Elijah standing beside Jesus. They stand next to him as men who have also known the wilderness. Also endured suffering. Also experienced the rejection of the very people they were called to lead.

How Jesus must have longed to step off that mountain and go with these kindred spirits back to heaven, to return home to his Father and to the honor that was rightfully his. He could have been swept from earth as Elijah had been by a chariot of fire. He could have been delivered as Moses had been by a miraculous exodus.

But no chariot comes to whisk him away from his circumstances. No miracles come to provide a way out of his suffering.

How ironic, the three of them standing together. He who is the fulfillment of the Law and Prophets stands between the greatest lawgiver and the greatest prophet, to be filled *by them*. Encouraged *by them*. Strengthened *by them*.

The Savior needs all the strength and encouragement they have to give, for the reality of his death weighs on him heavily. And so for him this moment on the mountain is a sacrament from heaven. A taste of the glory that awaits him. A sip of the joy that will be his at the messianic feast. The sacrament not only whets his appetite for those days but sustains him for the days ahead.

But the sacredness of that moment is interrupted by a clumsy attempt to memorialize the moment.

"Lord, it is good for us to be here. If you wish, I will put up three shelters—one for you, one for Moses and one for Elijah."

Once again Peter gets in the way. And once again, in so many words, he is asked to step aside.

"This is my Son, whom I love; with him I am well pleased."

The mountain quakes as an aftershock from those words, and the disciples tumble to the ground. But the words have a different effect on Jesus, a settling effect. They were what he needed to hear three years ago before he faced the temptations of the wilderness. And they are what he needs to hear now before he faces the tortures of the cross.

He needs to hear those words, but maybe more than the words themselves, he needs to hear the voice. That familiar inflection. That fatherly tone. So rich and resonant. So full of eternity. Just the sound of his Father's voice infuses him with strength.

The voice returns, rending the veil of mountain air like a stab of lightning.

"Listen to him!"

The imperative is punctuated with a clap of thunder that rolls over the disciples and presses them harder to the ground.

The message Jesus has been trying to get them to hear is a crucial one: he must suffer and die, and they must brace themselves for that reality. He told them this before they climbed the mountain, but Peter refused to listen. He would tell them again after they made their descent. Then they will listen. And understand. And grieve.

As the disciples cower in the dirt, Jesus touches them and tells them to get up. Just as the sun emerges from the clouds after a thunderstorm to spread its warmth upon the shivering earth, the touch of the Savior's hand radiates assurance to the trembling disciples.

"Don't be afraid."

They look up. Moses is gone. Elijah is gone. The cloud

and the light are gone. They see only Jesus. Only *his* face. Only *his* eyes.

Years later Peter and John would write about what they saw that day.

"We have seen his glory," John would testify. For him that moment underscored the Savior's deity. For him the glory he saw was like the Shekinah glory within the tabernacle, except this tabernacle was not made of animal skin and wooden poles; it was made of human flesh and bone.

"We were eyewitnesses of his majesty," Peter would one day recount. And for him this moment was a miraculous sign that authenticated the prophetic word about the coming kingdom.

James was the only one of the three who didn't record the event. Maybe he had intended to, but he was the first of the twelve to be martyred, and his life was cut short. Although he didn't write about this intense moment, it made an indelible impression and undoubtedly sustained him during his final hour of suffering . . . just as it had sustained his Savior who went before him.

On that day on the mountain the disciples saw Jesus in a way they had never seen him before. Before that day, they saw themselves on a fast camel bound for glory, their minds dizzy with thoughts of greatness in the coming kingdom. What they didn't see was that the road to glory passed through the tunnel of suffering.

Jesus asked his disciples to follow him through that tunnel, which connected this life to the next. They would have to stoop to enter, and they would have to leave everything behind to squeeze through the narrow opening.

That's where the Transfiguration fits in.

It was, quite literally, the light at the end of the tunnel—a glimpse of the glory on the other side. The way to that glory is not a road around suffering but through it. And joy is found in the destination, not the detour.

It would be the reward of not only being with Christ but sharing his glory that would give the disciples the strength to crawl through that tunnel. So dazzling was that reward that whatever they had to go through, whatever they had to leave behind, paled by comparison.

But to share Christ's glory means we must first share his suffering. The cross comes before the crown; humiliation before exaltation.

And though Peter was slow in getting that message, he did listen that day on the mountain. Years later he wrote to those who were as confused as he once was regarding the role suffering plays in the drama of redemption:

"Dear friends, do not be surprised at the painful trial you are suffering, as though something strange were happening to you. But rejoice that you participate in the sufferings of Christ, so that you may be overjoyed when his glory is revealed."

That is the message of the Transfiguration—the joy that awaits us at the end. And that is what the Savior needed to hear . . . and to see . . . and to feel. For it was the joy set before him on that mountaintop that gave him the strength to make the descent to endure the cross.

PRAYER

 ear most glorious King,

Help me to see the magnitude of sacrifice in your descent from the mount of transfiguration to the valley of the shadow of death. From the pinnacle of exaltation to the tear-washed gullies of humiliation. From inexpressible glory to unspeakable shame.

You could so easily have stepped off that mountain to heaven, escorted by Moses and Elijah. You could have lived out your days in the serenity of that mountain-top. Spending time with those who were closest to you. Shielded from the anger of those who opposed you. Sequestered from the ragged fray of humanity that fringed the streets below.

But instead you chose to descend those slopes. Down to stitch up the strands of humanity that lay so threadbare on those streets. Down to offer your tender wrists to those terrible nails. Down to the coldness and aloneness in the pitch-black bowels of the earth.

Help me to see, O most glorious Lord, that this is the path to glory. That in shouldering my cross in this life, my neck is given the strength to wear a crown in the next. And that when my cross bends my back low, it is there I am given the humility to wear a crown without the risk of it going to my head.

I pray for the coming of the kingdom which offers that crown. May it come quickly.

Thank you for the way you saw Peter, who seemed to

say all the wrong things at all the wrong times and who seemed to step so often in places where even angels feared to tread. Thank you for seeing him not for who he was but for who he would one day become.

Grant me the grace, I pray, to see those around me with that kind of eyes.

Lift the veil, O Lord. Help me to see them in a different light, beyond the ordinariness of their earthly tent. Beyond the shabbiness. Beyond the hastily sewn patches on the exterior. Help me to see within that most holy place of their souls, and grant me a glimpse of the glory that might someday be theirs in heaven.

Help me to comprehend the message of the Transfiguration, a message so radiant with hope it can brighten any tunnel. No matter how long or how hard. No matter how dark or how cold or how lonely.

At all times, but especially in times of suffering, help me to fix my eyes on you, Lord Jesus, the author and perfecter of our faith, who for the joy set before you endured the cross. Help me to consider you who endured such opposition from sinful men, so that I will not grow weary and lose heart when it comes my turn to carry a cross. . . .

AN
INTENSE MOMENT
OUTSIDE
JERUSALEM

SCRIPTURE

After Jesus had said this, he went on ahead, going up to Jerusalem. As he approached Bethphage and Bethany at the hill called the Mount of Olives, he sent two of his disciples, saying to them, "Go to the village ahead of you, and as you enter it, you will find a colt tied there, which no one has ever ridden. Untie it and bring it here. If anyone asks you, 'Why are you untying it?' tell him, 'The Lord needs it.'"

Those who were sent ahead went and found it just as he had told them. As they were untying the colt, its owners asked them, "Why are you untying the colt?"

They replied, "The Lord needs it."

They brought it to Jesus, threw their cloaks on the colt and put Jesus on it. As he went along, people spread their cloaks on the road.

When he came near the place where the road goes down the Mount of Olives, the whole crowd of disciples began joyfully to praise God in loud voices for all the miracles they had seen:

"Blessed is the king who comes in the name of the Lord!"

"Peace in heaven and glory in the highest!"

Some of the Pharisees in the crowd said to Jesus, "Teacher, rebuke your disciples!"

"I tell you," he replied, "if they keep quiet, the stones will cry out."

As he approached Jerusalem and saw the city, he wept over it and said, "If you, even you, had only known on this day what would bring you peace—but now it is hidden from your eyes. The days will come upon you when your enemies will build an embankment against you and encircle you and hem you in on every side. They will dash you to the ground, you and the children within your walls. They will not leave one stone on another, because you did not recognize the time of God's coming to you."

Luke 19:28–44

MEDITATION

he Lord needs it." And without so much as a raised brow of resistance, the owners let them borrow it.

Here it is a colt Jesus borrows.

Before that it was a boat. And before that a boy's lunch. The one he borrowed as a platform for preaching; the other, as food for a miracle.

In a week it will be a grave he borrows. For even in death the Son of Man still has nowhere to lay his head.

Such irony. The one through whom all things came into being, himself has nothing. A king without so much as a colt to his name. Without even a denarius with which to rent one.

It is such a king who rides today toward Jerusalem. Seated not on a proud Arabian horse but on a borrowed little donkey. His legs dangling on either side. His feet almost dragging the ground.

It is an unkingly sight. Almost a comic sight. But this is how he comes. Meek and lowly. Without pomp. Without ceremony. Without even the slightest concern for appearances.

He comes the more difficult way to Jerusalem by the uphill route to the west. The road he travels is lined with people waiting like tiptoed children for a parade.

One of those waiting in line does something you would expect only from a child caught up in the excitement of the moment. He rushes toward Jesus, peels off his cloak, and spreads it before the young donkey.

As he scurries back in line, another man strips himself and lays his garment down.

Then another.

The childlike excitement spreads, and a surge of people fills the road. Men pulling off cloaks. Women spreading out shawls. Younger men climbing trees, tearing off palm fronds and olive branches and limbs of sweet-smelling balsam. Children picking handfuls of spring flowers and sprinkling them in the Savior's path.

As they do, the colt plods ahead one tentative step at a time, struggling under the unaccustomed weight. Jesus also struggles with the weight he carries. And the closer he comes to the holy city, the heavier that weight becomes.

He is so near to Jerusalem. Yet Jerusalem is so far from him. And the pain of that thought is almost too much for him to bear.

His burden is lightened, though, by the people lining the road, reaching out to him as he approaches, their hands an extension of their hearts. For they have seen his miracles. They have tasted something from heaven. Something from the King's own table. Something warm and sweet and good. They reach out to him like hungry children, children who could never again be satisfied with any other bread but his.

That is why they spread their garments before him and toss him their garlands of praise. His coming is a royal procession; their cloaks, a welcome for their king.

Until now Jesus has refused any attempts to make him king. When the feeding-of-the-five-thousand crowd wanted to crown him, he escaped to a quiet hillside. When his family challenged him one Passover to reveal himself to Jerusalem, he declined.

But this Passover is different. This Passover he comes to reveal himself. And he has picked a colt instead of a chariot to make sure Jerusalem understands that he is the King Zechariah foretold.

> Rejoice greatly, O Daughter of Zion!
> Shout, Daughter of Jerusalem!
> See, your king comes to you,
> righteous and having salvation,
> gentle and riding on a donkey,
> on a colt, the foal of a donkey.

In so coming Jesus forces the hand of the religious aristocracy. After this public act, they would have to cast a public vote. No more meetings behind closed doors. No more plotting in private. They would have to come out in the open. They would have to confess him or curse him. Crown him or kill him.

As the colt strains to crest the hill, a small corner of the city edges into view. To the people waiting on the downslope side, Jesus seems to rise out of the summit. "There he is!" someone yells, and the crowd showers Jesus with praise.

"Blessed is the king who comes in the name of the Lord!"

"Peace in heaven and glory in the highest!"

For some this is a spontaneous moment of worship. It comes without the prompting of a leader or the guiding of a liturgy. For their love is enough to lead them; their joy is enough of a guide.

But what is expressive for some is offensive for others.

The Pharisees are ruffled by this sudden flurry of emotion. They worry about what could happen if this type of emotionalism swept through the gates of Jerusalem. How it would disrupt the solemn Passover ceremonies. How it might whisk away impressionable pilgrims from their religious roots.

At least those are the concerns that surface as they talk to the people about the dangers of this religious renegade. Beneath the surface what each of them really worries about is that Jesus might call into question their motives and their integrity, make them look bad, undermine their authority among the people, threaten their job security.

For these reasons the sloshing joy of the crowd does not spill over to the Pharisees. Their hearts are not filled with joy but with judgment. And since the mouth speaks from that which fills the heart, their mouths do not overflow with worship but with rebuke.

For them, the crowd is misinformed; their emotion, misguided; their praise, a mistake.

A mistake they insist Jesus correct. But the correction he gives is aimed instead at the Pharisees, whose heads are full of theological hairs straining to be split.

How stubborn of them to stand silent when surrounded

by such worship. And how tragic. So much education; so little understanding. So much learning; so little life.

The lowly colt understands none of this. It knows only that the shift in weight going downhill is a relief. The relief is short-lived, though, for the road winds and mounts again steeply. As it levels out, the entire city ascends into view.

Surrounded by walls that are inset with watchtowers, the city graces Mount Zion like a tiara. It sparkles in the sun, its patchy overlay of gold and bronze throwing back light like the facets of royal gems.

Behind the walls are lush gardens and lavish palaces. There is Herod's palace, sentried with ranks of stone columns. There is the Fort of Antonia, garrisoned with regiments of mercenary soldiers. And there is the temple, set like the central jewel in Jerusalem's crown, with its looming symmetry and sharp angles of gleaming marble.

For every Jew who ever crested that hill it was a breathtaking sight. But for Jesus it is a panorama of pain.

He bursts into tears.

How long he cried or how hard, we are not told. But the word Luke uses is a strong one, used of convulsive sobbing. Not much is made of those tears. Luke notes them without comment. But much is there.

In them is distilled an eternity of grief.

And although we know something of the brimming surface of those tears, we know nothing of the depths from which they are drawn. Nothing of the pain that lies at the watery depths of his heart. Nothing of the sorrow. Or the sadness.

What dark thoughts billow within Jesus to produce this downpour of emotion? What chilling sight causes his feelings to condense into tears?

Who knows for sure? But who can blame him? He is going to his death. A horrible, shameful, humiliating death. He knows the pain will be unbearable.

He knows the cloaks of honor will lead to a cloak of dishonor. He knows the blessings outside the gates will change to curses within. He knows the hands of praise will become fists of punishment. He knows the reverently placed palms will become a mocking reed scepter.

But knowing all this, Jesus does not weep for himself. He weeps for Jerusalem.

"If you, even you, had only known on this day what would bring you peace—but now it is hidden from your eyes. The days will come upon you when your enemies will build an embankment against you and encircle you and hem you in on every side. They will dash you to the ground, you and the children within your walls. They will not leave one stone on another, because you did not recognize the time of God's coming to you."

Through a mist of remorse Jesus peers into Jerusalem's future. He sees legions of soldiers surrounding the city. Their swords drawn. Their battering rams positioned. Their catapults cocked and ready to heave boulders at the walls.

He sees the bloodshed. He hears the tortured cries. He feels the pain of manacles cutting the wrists of survivors.

According to Josephus, Titus besieged Jerusalem in A. D. 70 when it was full of Passover visitors. Roman troops surrounded the city and kept anyone from entering or leaving. Cut off from supplies, many of the Jews resorted to eating the leather on their belts and sandals. Many starved. By August soldiers stormed the city and tore down the temple. Those who escaped the sword fled to higher ground, but by September they too were defeated and the city destroyed. Over a million Jews died. Those who survived were enslaved.

How much future did Jesus see that day as he sat on the low back of that little donkey that clopped along the downhill road to Jerusalem? Just forty years? Or did he see further?

The Savior's tears are mentioned sparingly in the Scriptures, and then only in passing. He wept over a friend who died. And over a nation that, in its own way, had also died.

He called them both out of their tombs. Lazarus came forth. Jerusalem didn't.

And because she didn't, tombs would continue to chronicle the world's suffering.

PRAYER

ord Jesus,

Help me to understand the weight you carried on that long road to Jerusalem. How much destruction did you see beyond the rubble of the temple? How many nations did you see beating their plows into swords and their pruning hooks into spears? How many Stalins and Hitlers did you see gathering darkly on the political horizon?

How many genocides did you witness because there was no peace between nations? How many homicides, because there was no peace between neighbors? How many suicides, because there was no peace in the human heart?

How much racial hatred did you see with those tear-filled eyes? How much fighting under the banner of religion? How much injustice?

How much, Lord, *did* you see? How much did you feel? How many tears did those eyes of yours cry?

Help me to see, in the sometimes blinding fervor of patriotism, that you came because of your Father's love for the world. The whole world. That your tears were not just for Jerusalem but also for Rome. Not just for Gettysburg but also for Atlanta. Not just for Treblinka but also for Hiroshima.

I pray for that world which your Father cradles so closely to his heart. A world that is on the brink of breaking apart. A world that is war-torn and weary. A world that knows so little of the peace you have to offer.

Help me to know that peace, O Lord, especially in my suffering.

Help me to understand the dark secret of love, the secret that only suffering can reveal: that if I love long enough and deeply enough, someday my heart will be broken.

As yours was broken.

Isaiah prophesied you would live among us as a broken-hearted man, a man of sorrows, acquainted with grief.

Help me to realize there are things, like the fulfillment of Isaiah's prophecy, that can only come to pass through suffering. I know character is one of them. And compassion is another. What are the others, Lord? Show me, please, so my suffering might be easier to bear.

Help me to understand that there is a communion with you that can only be shared through the sacrament of tears. And that the elements of that eucharist come from the crushing experiences of life.

And as I bend my knees to partake of those elements, draw me close . . . hold me tight . . . give me peace. . . .

AN
INTENSE MOMENT
IN GETHSEMANE

SCRIPTURE

They went to a place called Gethsemane, and Jesus said to his disciples, "Sit here while I pray." He took Peter, James and John along with him, and he began to be deeply distressed and troubled. "My soul is overwhelmed with sorrow to the point of death," he said to them. "Stay here and keep watch."

Going a little farther, he fell to the ground and prayed that if possible the hour might pass from him. "Abba, Father," he said, "everything is possible for you. Take this cup from me. Yet not what I will, but what you will."

Then he returned to his disciples and found them sleeping. "Simon," he said to Peter, "are you asleep? Could you not keep watch for one hour? Watch and pray so that you will not fall into temptation. The spirit is willing, but the body is weak."

Once more he went away and prayed the same thing. When he came back, he again found them sleeping, because their eyes were heavy. They did not know what to say to him.

Returning the third time, he said to them, "Are you still sleeping and resting? Enough! The hour has come. Look, the Son of Man is betrayed into the hands of sinners. Rise! Let us go! Here comes my betrayer!"

Mark 14:32–42

MEDITATION

ethsemane is where we go when there's no place to go but God.

It is where Jesus goes the night of his betrayal. He has gone there often, so it will be the first place his betrayer looks. He knows that. And maybe that is *why* he goes.

Jesus leaves the warm, intimate setting of the upper room to lead his disciples down a shoulder of hill that crumbles into the Kidron Valley. A dewy chill clings to them in their descent. Above, a saucer of light spills over the temple walls, its pale milk flowing down the path to collect in the slurpy brook below.

It is midnight as they step over the bald rocks in the brook. On the other side they shake water from their sandals and pause as a Roman sentry calls out his watch.

To the disciples it is merely a rending of the silence and a reminder of the time. To Jesus it is a rending of his heart and a reminder that time is running out.

When the disciples look up, Jesus is several paces ahead. He stops in a grove of olive trees at the foot of Gethsemane. Though it will be May before the trees blossom, the scent of oil still lingers from the residue on the stone press from last autumn's harvest.

The breeze that brings this scent to them now sighs into silence. The twitching branches grow still. Some of the trees in this garden have waited with rooted patience over a thousand years for this moment. And before them, every tree since Eden. Each branch holding on to the bud of a promise. Clinging to the hope that in their lifetime the Messiah will come and lead the creation back to Paradise.

Tonight he comes.

He brings with him his closest disciples. He knows the others are tired, but these three he brings with him; these three he needs as a cloak against the night. He stations them nearby to watch and to pray.

As he makes his way to the heart of the garden, the weight of his destiny bears down on him. He stops to rest his forearm against a large branch. For generations the olive branch has been a symbol of peace. But not tonight. Not for Jesus.

For the disciples, though, the garden offers a quiet place to rest. They huddle together as a fortress against sleep, but the day has been long and supper is settling in their stomachs, and one by one they fall victim to the night.

Alone in the clearing, Jesus falls to his knees, then to the ground. Seen through the foliage, this darkly mottled portrait drips with intensity. And humanity. For Jesus was never more human than he is now. Never more weak. Never more sad.

And yes, never more afraid.

He clutches the mane of grass as if to rein in the runaway terror. He writhes on the ground, his agony reflected in the twisted trunks of the onlooking trees. He claws the ground, groping for its embrace.

But there is no embrace.

There is only silence and darkness and the cold, hard ground.

The angels watch all this but are restricted to the shadows. Legions of them craning their necks. Aching to help. Watching as Jesus wrestles in the dark night that has fallen upon his soul.

He wrestles in prayer. But his prayer is no well-constructed sonnet, whispered with composure. His words are the shards of a broken heart. And they shred his soul on the way up.

As he pushes the words into the night, his wrinkled brow wrings sweat from his face. And he looks least likely of all to be the one who will lead the creation back to Paradise.

He who once towered over his opposition like the cedars of Lebanon now lies folded on the ground, a bent reed of a man. Eden's only hope lying in the dirt among so many fallen twigs.

But Jesus gets up. Wipes the gritty sweat from his face. Returns to his disciples. Desperately needing their companionship, their encouragement, their prayers.

But the disciples are asleep.

He starts to chide them. But he knows the weakness of the flesh as well as the willingness of the spirit, and he can't bring himself to be hard on them.

He returns to the clearing with the fateful realization

that this is a place where he must wrestle alone. Where he must sweat alone. And pray alone.

"Abba, Father."

His words are underscored with sobs. "Everything is possible for you." And punctuated with long periods of silence.

"Take this cup from me."

The Father's heart breaks over what he sees, what he hears. His own son, groveling in the dirt. His *only* son, crying in the dark like a lost little boy.

"Abba."

And what father wouldn't answer a request like that?

> "Which of you, if his son asks for bread, will give him a stone? Or if he asks for a fish, will give him a snake? If you, then, though you are evil, know how to give good gifts to your children, how much more will your Father in heaven give good gifts to those who ask him!"

But on this dark night good gifts from heaven don't come. Neither does an answer.

The only answer that comes is voiced though the events of that night and the next day. The son is betrayed, deserted, arrested, denied, beaten, tried, mocked, and crucified.

An apparent stone instead of the requested bread; a snake instead of the fish.

"Abba." The cry is weaker now.

For a moment an unseen gate is opened, and an angel is allowed to step from the shadows. He enters the arena not to save Jesus from his suffering but to strengthen him so he can endure it.

Jesus pushes himself up from the ground and lifts his eyes towards heaven.

"Yet not what I will, but what you will."

His hands are no longer clutching the grass in despair. They are no longer clasping each other in prayer.

They are raised toward heaven.

Reaching not for bread or for fish or for any other good gift. Not even for answers.

But reaching for the cup from his Father's hand.

And though it is a terrible cup, brimming with the wrath of God for the ferment of sin from centuries past and centuries yet to come . . . and though it is a cup he fears . . . he takes it.

Because more than he fears the cup, he loves the hand from which it comes.

PRAYER

ear Man of Sorrows,

Thank you for Gethsemane. For a place to go when there's no place to go but God. For a place to pray. And to cry. And to find out who I really am underneath the rhetoric.

I know that sometime, somewhere, some type of Gethsemane awaits me. Just as it did you. I know that someday a dark night will fall upon my soul. Just as it did yours. But I shudder to think about it, about the darkness and the aloneness and the despair.

Prepare me for that dark night, Lord. Prepare me now by helping me realize that although Gethsemane is the most terrifying of places, it is also the most tranquil.

The terror comes in realizing I am not in control of my life or the lives of those I love. The tranquility comes in realizing that you are.

Help me when it is dark and I am alone and afraid. Help me to put my trembling hand in yours and trust you with my life. And with the lives of those I love.

Someday I know I will wrestle with circumstances that are beyond my control, that some sort of suffering will pin me to the cold, hard ground.

When that happens, Lord Jesus, help me to realize that the victories of heaven are the defeats of the human soul. And that my strength is not found in how courageously I struggle but in how completely I surrender. . . .

AN
INTENSE MOMENT
IN
ROMAN HANDS

SCRIPTURE

hen the Jews led Jesus from Caiaphas to the palace of the Roman governor. By now it was early morning, and to avoid ceremonial uncleanness the Jews did not enter the palace; they wanted to be able to eat the Passover. So Pilate came out to them and asked, "What charges are you bringing against this man?"

"If he were not a criminal," they replied, "we would not have handed him over to you."

Pilate said, "Take him yourselves and judge him by your own law."

"But we have no right to execute anyone," the Jews objected. This happened so that the words Jesus had spoken indicating the kind of death he was going to die would be fulfilled.

Pilate then went back inside the palace, summoned Jesus and asked him, "Are you the king of the Jews?"

"Is that your own idea," Jesus asked, "or did others talk to you about me?"

"Am I a Jew?" Pilate replied. "It was your people and your chief priests who handed you over to me. What is it you have done?"

Jesus said, "My kingdom is not of this world. If it were, my servants would fight to prevent my arrest by the Jews. But now my kingdom is from another place."

"You are a king, then!" said Pilate.

Jesus answered, "You are right in saying I am a king. In fact, for this reason I was born, and for this I came into the world, to testify to the truth. Everyone on the side of truth listens to me."

"What is truth?" Pilate asked. With this he went out again to the Jews and said, "I find no basis for a charge against him. But it is your custom for me to release to you one prisoner at the time of the Passover. Do you want me to release 'the king of the Jews'?"

They shouted back, "No, not him! Give us Barabbas!" Now Barabbas had taken part in a rebellion.

Then Pilate took Jesus and had him flogged. The soldiers twisted together a crown of thorns and put it on his head. They clothed him in a purple robe and went up to him again and again, saying, "Hail, king of the Jews!" And they struck him in the face.

Once more Pilate came out and said to the Jews, "Look, I am bringing him out to you to let you know that I find no basis for a charge against him." When Jesus came out wearing the crown of thorns and the purple robe, Pilate said to them, "Here is the man!"

As soon as the chief priests and their officials saw him, they shouted, "Crucify! Crucify!"

But Pilate answered, "You take him and crucify him. As for me, I find no basis for a charge against him."

The Jews insisted, "We have a law, and according to that law he must die, because he claimed to be the Son of God."

When Pilate heard this, he was even more afraid, and he went back inside the palace. "Where do you come from?" he asked Jesus, but Jesus gave him no answer. "Do you refuse to speak to me?" Pilate said. "Don't you realize I have power either to free you or to crucify you?"

Jesus answered, "You would have no power over me if it were not given to you from above. Therefore the one who handed me over to you is guilty of a greater sin."

From then on, Pilate tried to set Jesus free, but the Jews kept shouting, "If you let this man go, you are no friend of Caesar. Anyone who claims to be a king opposes Caesar."

When Pilate heard this, he brought Jesus out and sat down on the judge's seat at a place known as the Stone Pavement (which in Aramaic is Gabbatha). It was the day of Preparation of Passover Week, about the sixth hour.

"Here is your king," Pilate said to the Jews.

But they shouted, "Take him away! Take him away! Crucify him!"

"Shall I crucify your king?" Pilate asked.

"We have no king but Caesar," the chief priests answered.

Finally Pilate handed him over to them to be crucified.

John 18:28–19:16

MEDITATION

nder Roman jurisdic-
tion, executions by the ruling council of the Sanhedrin
were outlawed. That's why the religious leaders brought
Jesus to Pilate. If found guilty under Roman law, he *could* be
executed. And what's more, the dirty work would fall to
the hands of the military.

The military was made up of brutal men born of brutal
times, weaned on the cruelties of the Colosseum, where
gladiators fought to the death and troublemakers were
thrown to the lions. The cruelty of these men defies
description. The horrors are too horrible for words. For
them torture was entertainment; the suffering of others
their sport.

Though himself a cruel man, Pilate is also a careful
man. Always calculating his next move. Always weighing
it against any consequences to his career. For now, his
career has placed him in the position of Procurator of Judea.
A job he disdains. He has no respect for the Jews over
whom he rules. Or for their beliefs. Or for their convic-
tions. He defers to them only when it is expedient.

On one such occasion he brought idolatrous images of
the emperor into the holy city, only to face five days of
impassioned Jewish resistance. He threatened the Jews with
death, but they stood their ground. On the sixth day, fear-
ing political repercussions, he relented and removed the
offending images.

On another occasion he proposed an aqueduct to
improve the water supply, but riots broke out when the Jews

learned he siphoned off money from the temple treasury to finance it. Though the uprising was silenced by Roman swords, Pilate learned to tread lightly over the will of the Jewish people.

Which is why he tiptoes around the trial of this particular Jew, this Jesus, this enigma that stands before him now. Jesus admits to the accusation against him. That he is a king. In the wake of silence created by that admission, Pilate circles Jesus, studying him.

He is nothing like a king, and yet . . . and yet something about him . . . something in his eyes . . . a look. A look that troubles Pilate. A look he can't explain. A look he fears.

Jesus looks him in the eyes, and beyond his eyes to his fears, and beyond his fears to the far reaches of his soul. "My kingdom is not of this world. If it were, my servants would fight to prevent my arrest by the Jews. But now my kingdom is from another place."

"Aha! So you admit it. You are a king, then!"

"You are right in saying I am a king. In fact, for this reason I was born, and for this I came into the world, to testify to the truth. Everyone on the side of truth listens to me."

Pilate's thoughts race in all directions. To Rome. To Jerusalem. And back again to Rome. Finally they come to a halt at the place of his conscience. But there they find no rest. Only questions.

"What is truth?"

Pilate's question is answered with silence. The question swings around and catches hold like a grappling hook onto the unscalable cliffs of his heart. He turns from Jesus and walks out onto his porch to address the people, walking gingerly between the confines of his own conscience and the coercions of the crowd.

In keeping with holiday tradition, he offers them the release of a prisoner, any prisoner. And in his heart the prisoner he hopes they choose is Jesus.

It is not. And once again the fateful choice falls to him.

He turns from the crowd. Picking his way carefully through the tangle of alternatives, he decides to have Jesus flogged. *Maybe that will satisfy them,* he thinks. *Maybe then they'll back down.* And so he gives the order, then retreats to his chambers to give his conscience a rest.

Jesus is taken away and stripped and made to kneel before a three-foot pillar with iron rings embedded in each side. Guards take his wrists, tie them with rope, and cinch them to the rings.

A whip is used to mete out the punishment. From its wooden handle nine leather cords extend sinuously. Attached to the cords are bits of bone, small links of metal chain, and other sharp objects.

The executioner takes the whip and stands six feet behind the prisoner. He works his wrist, and nine leather snakes slither over the floor. Then he spreads his legs, positioning his feet for traction.

With a flick of his wrist, he charms the leather to rise.

Flinging the cords behind him, his rippling right arm then snaps them forward. They strike, sinking their fangs into Jesus' ribs. The burly arm jerks back the leather, tearing off pieces of flesh and spattering ovals of blood onto the floor.

The bite of the whip sends tremors of pain through every nerve in Jesus' body. The pain travels all the way to the nerves in his lips, which quiver, but which do not cry out.

Another swing, and the flailing cords not only wrap themselves around Jesus' back but around his arms and neck and head.

Tributaries of pain pool in his eyes.

Another lash, and the skin on his shoulders opens up, exposing a jagged valley of muscle, and at the bottom of that valley, the glistening white of bone.

Silent tears spill down his face.

By the time the flogging is over, the skin on the Savior's back is eaten away. Welted trails of blood map the cruelty on the rest of his body. The two guards who brought him pick him up and take him back to Pilate.

But Pilate has been detained with other business, with decrees Herod wants him to sign and budgets he wants him to approve. Jesus is brought to a holding area.

The area is an expansive hall in the Praetorium, where hundreds of men are gathered. Military men. Men with stubbled beards and pockmarked faces and skin notched with the scars of battle. Rough-hewn men quarried from the soulless stone of surrounding provinces. Provinces that hated Jews.

The room into which this solitary Jew is now led is thick with these soulless men; the air thick with their sweat, their coarse talk, and their foul-smelling breath.

Jesus' hands—hands that once reached out to touch lepers and to stroke the hair of children—are cuffed in rope. Guards shouldered on either side parade him around the perimeter of soldiers.

The soldiers know little about Jesus, except the rumor of his claim to be some sort of king. As they stop their activity to eye the rumored king, the smell of sport in the air comes to them strongly, irresistibly. Crouching on eager haunches, they approach him. Like a pack of wolves they salivate for a taste of fresh blood.

A guard cuts the rope from the prisoner's wrists. Weary from the loss of sleep and light-headed from the loss of blood, Jesus collapses. A voice howls, "Strip him!" And a few of the soldiers pounce and pull Jesus to his feet, ripping the blood-soaked garment off his back.

He stands naked before the bared teeth and bristled backs of his enemies. Their predatory instincts push them to laugh and point and shout catcalls.

He not only stands naked and silent before his shearers, he stands alone. There is no one to defend him. No one to shield him from their stares. No one to protect him from their savagery.

A man shoves him a stool. "Your throne, O King. Sit."

95

As the half-conscious Jesus stiffly moves, the man hurls expletives in his face and shouts, "I said sit down!"

When Jesus starts to sit, the stool is pulled out from under him. The room erupts in laughter.

The soldier extends a hand. Weakly Jesus reaches for it. As he does, the soldier balls his other hand into a fist and hits him. Amid the raucous laughter, amid the pool of blood streaming from his nose, Jesus lies motionless. With his face against the flagstone floor, Jesus closes his eyes. For a moment his swelling face finds mercy in the cool of the stone.

But only for a moment.

Another soldier nudges him with his boot and extends a hand. Through eyelids swollen and slitted, Jesus looks up. As he takes the hand, the man fakes a punch. Jesus flinches. And another round of laughter fills the circle.

A couple of soldiers hoist the battered prisoner onto the stool. One of them prostrates himself. "A gift from a loyal subject," he says and then rises with an uppercut, tearing the ligaments in Jesus' jaw from their hinges and sending him and the stool reeling backwards.

They drape a deep red cape around his shoulders, which blots the spillage of blood and dyes the cloth a more somber shade. They put him back on the stool and place a tall reed in his hand. "Your scepter, your Majesty."

Another soldier has taken a strand of thorns from the tinder box and woven it into a wreath. "King's gotta have a crown." And he mashes the three-inch thorns into Jesus' scalp. Jesus grimaces as God's curse on Eden comes to curse him back.

Another man yanks the reed from Jesus' hand and slaps it across his head, driving the thorns deeper. Each puncture leaks a line of blood. Each pulsebeat sends trickles of the Savior's life ebbing down his face.

"Hail, King of the Jews!" shouts the commanding officer, and the entire cohort kneels. But instead of tossing the king garlands of praise, the soldiers dredge up phlegm from the raspy depths of their throats and toss that.

The king is pelted with a volley of spit. Then another. And another. Until at last he is drenched with their disdain.

Word comes to the guards that Pilate is ready for the prisoner, so they lead him back to the hall of judgment—a judgment Pilate is reluctant to make. He believes Jesus is innocent. But he has to convince the crowds.

Pilate brings Jesus in full view of those crowds, hoping the pitiful sight will evoke a sense of pity.

Pilate announces, "Here is the man!" *The one you want to crucify. Look at him now.*

Behold the face.

Behold the back.

Behold the blood and the bruises and the broken heart.

Behold the God who became flesh and allowed *this* to be done to it.

"Here is your king." And with those words Pilate says

more than he knows. Had he known what is truth, he would have thrown himself at Jesus' feet and surrendered his crown, his career, his life.

But Jesus is a sad caricature of a king, and what rational man could believe that royalty would come packaged like this?

So the crown goes unsurrendered. And the career. And the life. And so goes the crowd of rational men, who refuse not only to submit to their king but to show him even a shred of mercy.

"Crucify him!"

"Crucify him!"

"Crucify him!"

The words come as waves of hate, one after the other, surging louder and louder until at last they crest and come crashing down. Pilate has faced these waves before. He has felt their fury, and he knows better than to stand against them. Even so, he tries one more time to turn the tide.

"Shall I crucify your king?"

"We have no king but Caesar," reply the chief priests in the front row, and their countermove wedges Pilate into a political corner, a corner from which there is no retreat. If word ever reached Rome that he freed a rival to the Emperor . . . The very thought sends shudders up his spine.

This isn't Rome's business, he says to himself. *And it certainly isn't worth risking a riot over. Or a career.*

So, in a politically expedient move, he approaches a laver and dips his hands into the water. In one cleansing gesture he appeases his conscience: "I am innocent of this man's blood." In another he dries his hands and appeases the crowd: "It is your responsibility!"

But the crowd has no conscience. "Let his blood be on us and our children!"

The words ring in Pilate's ears as he pauses. He looks at Christ. He looks at the crowd.

Slowly, so very slowly, he returns the towel to the washstand.

And walks away.

PRAYER

 King,

Who came to your own people in such quiet and humble and unsuspecting ways, but who your own did not receive.

How that must have broken your heart.

And how it must break again and again—even this day, even as I pray—the many times you come and are not received. Not recognized for who you are, let alone worshiped. Not loved. Or embraced. Or served.

Forgive me for all the times *I* have not received you, Jesus. For all the times *I* have rejected you. For all the times *I* have broken your heart.

Touch my heart, O Heart that was once so wounded and is so wounded still, and make it sensitive to the many ways you come to me. To the quiet ways I have to quiet myself to hear. To the humble ways I have to humble myself to see. To the unsuspecting ways I have to expect if I ever am able to receive.

Give me eyes to see royalty beneath the most incomprehensible of robes. Help me to see your hunger in the face of the poor, your sores on the body of the sick, your callouses on the feet of the homeless, your words in the mouths of babes.

Help me to realize what Pilate failed to. That you are the truth. And more than the truth. That you are King.

I am so sorry, Jesus, so very, very sorry for all you suffered at the hands of those you loved so deeply.

Forgive me for the part that I have played in your suffering. For my fingerprints were on those hands that hurt you. Something of me was in them who did such unspeakable things to you. And something of them is in me. Even now.

Help me to realize who I am apart from you. And who I am *because* of you, Lord Jesus, my King. . . .

AN
INTENSE MOMENT
AT GOLGOTHA

SCRIPTURE

Two other men, both criminals, were also led out with him to be executed. When they came to the place called the Skull, there they crucified him, along with the criminals—one on his right, the other on his left. Jesus said, "Father, forgive them, for they do not know what they are doing." And they divided up his clothes by casting lots.

The people stood watching, and the rulers even sneered at him. They said, "He saved others; let him save himself if he is the Christ of God, the Chosen One."

The soldiers also came up and mocked him. They offered him wine vinegar and said, "If you are the king of the Jews, save yourself."

There was a written notice above him, which read: THIS IS THE KING OF THE JEWS.

One of the criminals who hung there hurled insults at him: "Aren't you the Christ? Save yourself and us!"

Luke 23:32–39

MEDITATION

t will be the last temptation of Christ.

And the greatest.

In the first temptation Luke's account ends on a foreboding note. "When the devil had finished all this tempting, he left him until an opportune time."

The words foreshadow a sequel to that great dual in the wilderness. But the second grab for Jesus' soul would have to be more strategically planned than the first. Satan knows this. The setting would have to be different. Starker. More desolate. And the timing, it would have to be different too.

It would have to be, as Luke suggests, a more *opportune time*. The word he uses is used elsewhere in Scripture of a time when fruit is heavy on the branch. A time ripe for picking. A harvest time.

The time of Satan's first temptation was when Christ's ministry was just beginning to bloom, when all looked hopeful. He knows if he comes again it would have to be a time when the bloom was off the branch, when all hope was gone.

That time is now.

The ministry is dead. And so almost is Jesus. He has suffered the loss of sleep, the loss of blood, and the loss of his friends. He was never more tired than he is now. Never more weak. Never more alone.

Satan knows the time is opportune. He has watched

from the corners of the upper room and waited in the shadows of Gethsemane. He has witnessed the betrayals and the trials, the mockings and the beatings. He knows. The soul of Christ has never been more ripe for the picking. Or more within his reach.

So he comes this one last time. Rubbing his hands for one last try. He approaches the tree in the middle. Reaching for the branch that is heavy with fruit. Straining to grab it before it falls into the hands of the Father.

The setting for this final temptation is a chalky knoll just outside Jerusalem's northern wall. Scooped with shallow caverns, the rounded hill looks grim and ominous and well-fitted to its name: Golgotha—"the place of the skull."

The skull stares away from the city, its stone gaze unmoved by the vultures and the crows and the other winged scavengers that stilt across its brow, pecking around for remains of the dead.

Three vertical beams are staked to the top of that hill, standing tall and unshaded in the morning sun. Like soldiers after reveille, standing at attention, awaiting the day's assignment.

The assignment for today is two robbers and a religious zealot.

This unlikely trio has led an unceremonious procession through the narrow city streets, shouldering their crossbeams as they stumbled over cobblestones.

But one of those times Jesus stumbled, he didn't get up. He was yelled at and kicked, but still he did not get up. A stranger was yanked from the sidewalk of gawkers and forced to carry his wood the rest of the way.

Now that they have trudged to the top of Golgotha, they drop their wooden beams. A ruffled assortment of feathers flaps back a few yards, the birds seeming to resent the intrusion. The prisoners are exhausted. Slick with sweat. Fresh blood oozing from their wounds. And the chirping birds form little conclaves of curiosity to study them.

One by one the prisoners are muscled to the ground and stretched across their crossbeams. The first thief struggles, but a handful of soldiers subdues him, sitting on him as the spiker does his work. He screams as the spikes impale his wrists. Two raps on one arm. Two more on the other.

Seeing this, hearing this, the other prisoner struggles even more desperately. But the guards subdue him too. Two raps. Then two more. And the uprising is put down.

They have saved Jesus for last. The soldiers stretch his arms across the coarse-grained wood. A soldier straddles his chest. Two others straddle his arms. Two others, his legs. They are used to the fitful resistance of condemned men. But this condemned man throws no fit, offers no resistance.

The spiker bends on one knee, the pockets of his leather apron bulging with nails, an iron-headed mallet filling his hand. He places the spike just below Jesus' wrist. The clank of metal echoes off the stone walls. One sharp rap to pene-trate the arm. One more to penetrate the wood. One rap on the other arm. Then another. And the job is done.

One by one the crossbeams are lifted into position. Four

107

soldiers lift Jesus' crossbeam and two steady his feet. Two others hoist it with ropes that run through a groove in the upright timber. The spikes scrape against the bones in his wrists, and the shifting weight of his body tears the skin and muscles in his arms. But he does not cry out. He buries a moan instead deep within his chest.

A soldier on a ladder steadies the crossbeam into the notch of the upright. As the beams are jostled into position, they rasp the open wounds on Jesus' back. The pain is excruciating, but the only anesthetic is the gritting of his teeth.

The bored holes in each beam are aligned, and a peg is driven through both to join the timbers. Once the crossbeam is secure, Christ's right leg is pulled over the left, and the spiker drives a single nail through both feet. His face winces to record how far the pain has traveled, and how deep. He opens his eyes and sees a few soldiers and the spiker milling around below.

"Father, forgive them—"

The three words impale them as forcefully as the three spikes they used to impale him. They all look up, transfixed, as Jesus finishes his prayer.

"—for they do not know what they are doing."

Not only does Jesus ask his Father to forgive them, he offers a kind word in their behalf, explaining their behavior.

The calloused ears of these soldiers have heard all kinds of words on that hill. All kinds. And in every language.

But they have never heard words like these. Never like these. Not once.

Until now.

A chasm of silence opens between the men, separating them from each other. An awkward moment for men used to loud talk and coarse language. In the quiet of that moment Jesus closes his eyes.

The silence below him is bridged by a few feeble planks of conversation. "What about his tunic?" asks one. "A shame to cut it up," says another. "Worth more in one piece."

The garment perhaps was woven by his mother. And if not by her, at least by somebody who loved him. The soldiers value it because it is seamless, not because it is his or because of the labor of love that it is.

And so dice are pulled from a pocket. "Winner takes all." A circle forms. After a few rolls they seem back to their old selves. The losers cursing. The winner bragging.

As the soldiers return to their stations, Satan returns to his.

He is more cunning this time around. Instead of coming out in the open, he voices his temptations through the traffic of onlookers passing by the cross. They are his mouthpiece, sounding almost as an echo from those windswept hills in the wilderness three and a half years ago.

There is a certain schizophrenia in Satan's strategy. The serpent of old coils to strike, yet he knows the heel he strikes could crush him if he's not careful. He delights in seeing God's Son suffer, yet he fears what that suffering could accomplish. So one last time this cold-blooded adversary slithers toward the Son of God with hissing contempt.

The first temptation comes through the religious leaders. Feeling the nearness of their victory, they pack around the cross like jackals cornering a crippled gazelle. Their sneering lips showing savage teeth. Their biting remarks showing a thirst for blood.

"He saved others; let him save himself *if* he is the Christ of God, the Chosen One."

Jesus could do that—save himself and show the religious establishment that he truly was the Messiah. The Chosen One. The promised seed of Eve through whom the curse of Eden would be reversed. The promised seed of Abraham through whom the entire earth would be blessed. The promised heir of David's throne through whom the kingdom of God would come.

So many promises converge at this cross. And maybe, maybe there was still a chance, even at this late hour, that they could come true . . .

If only Jesus would save himself.

But their sneers are met only with silence. And soon the rulers lose their taste for blood and leave.

Sometime later, soldiers making their rounds stop at Christ's cross. They plop a bucket of sour wine on the ground and dip a sponge in it. They stick the sponge on a hyssop branch and use it to mop his wounds. His body writhes at the briny sting of alcohol.

The soldiers laugh as they sponge the prisoner down, betting they can get the holy man to curse his god, and if not his god, at least the day of his birth.

But he curses neither.

They push the sponge at his mouth. But he turns his face away.

Then one of the gutter-mouthed men curses Jesus and mocks him with a second temptation.

"If you are the king of the Jews, save yourself."

Jesus opens his swollen eyes and sees the blur of men below. What stories these eyewitnesses could tell their superiors if he did come down and save himself. What evangelists they would make. What revival would break out in Rome. How Christianity would flourish under government protection. How legislation would change under Christian influence. It would be an unparalleled opportunity. . . .

If only Jesus would save himself.

But Jesus doesn't save himself. He doesn't even save his dignity. He offers no defense. Makes no reply. Seeing little sport in his silence, the soldiers move on to the next cross.

But Satan does not move with them. He stays to work out another strategy.

Since he couldn't appeal to Christ through the religious leaders or the Roman soldiers, maybe he could reach him through one of the robbers. Since Christ knew what pain the man was going through, maybe the dying man's suffering would soften him.

111

"Aren't you the Christ? Save yourself and us!"

Slowly Jesus turns his head to see the man who insulted him. He sees eyes that are lit with anger. Anger at life for bringing him there. Anger at Rome for putting him there. Anger at Jesus for leaving him there.

How simple it would be for Jesus to ease the burn in the soul that enflames this man's eyes. He has done it so many times before. He thinks of the Gerasene demoniac and the fire he extinguished when he expelled the demons from the desert of that man's soul. He thinks, too, of the woman at the well and how the living water he offered quenched the desperate thirst in her soul.

He can stop the fire in this man's soul too. And the fever in his wounds. And in the man next to him. . . .

If only Jesus would save himself.

And us.

But Jesus knows something the man hanging next to him doesn't. He knows he can choose one or the other. He can save himself. Or he can save us. But he can't do both.

In spite of how much pain he was in. In spite of how tired he was. How weak. And how alone. He had the strength to choose us.

It was the struggle of the wilderness that prepared Jesus for the sufferings of the cross. Giving him the strength not to give in . . . the courage not to come down . . . and the selflessness to save us instead of himself.

PRAYER

ear Jesus of Nazareth,

Who is King not only of the Jews, but of every thought and impulse of my life.

Rule over those thoughts, Lord Jesus, and over those impulses. They are so prone to rebel. So quick to run riot. So weak to resist temptation.

Strengthen me when I am tempted, especially with the temptations that come during suffering. They are so seductive. And I am so susceptible to their allure.

Help me to discern the strategies of the enemy, who so often voices his appeals through the mouths of others. They are so subtle, and sometimes I am so unsuspecting.

Deliver me from the temptation to protect myself from pain, and from the temptation to point my finger at the ones inflicting it. From the selfishness of wanting to save myself. And from the bitterness of wanting to blame others.

Help me to learn from the example of your suffering. That forgiveness is the power to resist bitterness. And surrender, the power to resist selfishness.

Help me to surrender to the daily crosses in my life. Give me the strength to shoulder the beam, to submit to the nails, to be silent before the abuse.

Help me to bear antagonism without anger, insult without indignation, ridicule without retaliation.

Help me to understand the nature and purpose of pain. If it is the chisel that crafts our character—chipping away until you are formed in us—then if I avoid pain, I also avoid the person the Father would have me to be.

Help me to someday become that person, Lord. Give me the strength to hold on to that which now may seem most painful but in the end will turn out to be that which best serves my soul.

And remind me, Lord, when I can't hold on any longer, that the terrifying being who wrestled with Jacob in the dark turned out to be, in the dawn, an angel . . . an angel who had the power to bestow on him a blessing. . . .

ANOTHER INTENSE MOMENT AT GOLGOTHA

SCRIPTURE

From the sixth hour until the ninth hour darkness came over all the land. About the ninth hour Jesus cried out in a loud voice, *"Eloi, Eloi, lama sabachthani?"*—which means, "My God, my God, why have you forsaken me?"

When some of those standing there heard this, they said, "He's calling Elijah."

Immediately one of them ran and got a sponge. He filled it with wine vinegar, put it on a stick, and offered it to Jesus to drink. The rest said, "Now leave him alone. Let's see if Elijah comes to save him."

And when Jesus had cried out again in a loud voice, he gave up his spirit.

At that moment the curtain of the temple was torn in two from top to bottom. The earth shook and the rocks split. The tombs broke open and the bodies of many holy people who had died were raised to life. They came out of the tombs, and after Jesus' resurrection they went into the holy city and appeared to many people.

When the centurion and those with him who were guarding Jesus saw the earthquake and all that had happened, they were terrified, and exclaimed, "Surely he was the Son of God!"

Matthew 27:45–54

MEDITATION

The centurion was king of the hill. But Golgotha was a small hill. And a hill nobody else wanted.

For a career soldier like he was, it was a low rung on the career ladder. But it was a step up from his last assignment and a step he would have to take if he wanted to move up.

He surveys the crosses branding the morning sky, making sure the job has been done right, checking to see if the nails are still holding. He stops to read the gypsum plaque above the head of the prisoner in the middle: "JESUS OF NAZARETH. THIS IS THE KING OF THE JEWS."

Jesus has hung beneath that indictment since nine this morning. His legs are cramping now, his back throbbing. His arms burn, and his tendons are torn from the sockets in his shoulders.

The centurion is intrigued by how this prisoner seems to gather his pain and hold it, keeping it to himself. *Why?* he wonders. *Why doesn't he suffer like the others, cursing and screaming and lashing out?*

He eyes the deposed king enthroned before him. Wonders how he ended up here. Exiled to this hill. He studies him, searching his eyes. Hoping to see something in them, find something, a clue maybe. But a curtain is drawn over the mystery as Jesus closes his eyes.

It is noon now, and the sun should be at full flame, burning off the shadows. But it isn't.

The centurion angles his eyes to see the sky ripening

from blue to indigo to violet and finally to black. Strange. It isn't an eclipse. Not a dust storm. Or cloudbank. More like an enveloping gloom.

The raven-colored darkness wings its way across the land, leaving behind it a chill. The people grow cold, and some of them huddle together. Others grow scared, thinking it a bad omen.

And so the crowd on the hill thins. But the darkness only thickens. For three hours the sun refuses to come out, almost as if it couldn't bear to look anymore. Heaven too, it seems, has looked away.

The sin of the world is settling on the Savior's shoulders. If he is to pay its penalty, he must bear its consequences, all of its consequences, including the most severe:

The abandonment of God.

Jesus has known the abandonment of his family, of his friends, and of his countrymen. But he has never known this kind of abandonment. He and his Father have always existed together as one, so eternally close that now, when fellowship between them is severed, the pain in the soul of the Son is like an amputation without anesthesia.

That is the pain he feels as he cries out:

"My God, my God, why have you forsaken me?"

He cries out "my God" rather than "my Father," so wide is the chasm separating them now. The chasm is a sentient one, and Jesus feels it. As the darkness deepens, the chasm widens, each widening a tearing of the ligaments of his soul.

These three hours are the dregs of the cup given Jesus in Gethsemane. And the fate of humanity comes down to this one final, bitter mouthful of suffering that only God's Son can swallow.

And swallowing it, he slumps into unconsciousness. He stays that way until a javelin of pain is sent flying into his shoulder, waking him with a start. His fever has worsened. His eyes burn. His throat is parched, his tongue thick and pasted down.

"I thirst."

The words trudge across his broken lips, weary and sun-stricken. He wants something to drink not so much to quench his thirst as to clear his throat. He has something else to say, and he wants to make sure everybody hears it, and hears it clearly.

A sponge of sour wine is poled up to him. He bites it, and wine channels down the sides of his mouth. What little he swallows mixes its blessings on the way down, stinging and soothing.

For three small words Jesus raises himself from the nails one last time. He takes a deep breath, then bequeaths these words as the legacy of his life.

"It is finished."

The cry is a cry of victory as the Son crosses the finish line. The race he came to earth to run is over. And he is just an exhausted stride away from falling into his Father's arms.

His head eases back against the wood. His eyes close. He feels the pain leaving him. He sees his Father's outstretched arms. He calls to him:

"Father, into your hands I commit my spirit."

And then he died. He died as he lived, in the affectionate embrace of his Father. His last act, an act of surrender. His last words, a prayer.

The centurion was used to watching men die. But none of them died like this. Not like this. He wonders who this man under the gypsum plaque was. Jesus the Nazarene? King of the Jews? Who?

While he wonders, the ground shudders beneath his feet. Suddenly the earth groans with deep abradings of rock. Soldiers are thrown staggering to the ground. People running for their lives, praying, screaming, falling down.

Crosses sway in their stone sockets. Nails tearing flesh. Screams knifing air. Boulders tumbling, crashing. Stones sealing tombs shaken open; the dead shaken to life.

The curtain separating the sanctuary from the Most Holy Place in the temple is torn from top to bottom, as if a mournful Father's hands reached down and rent it.

And then, the earth calms. First from its trembling. Then from its shivering. Then altogether.

The centurion pulls himself up from the terror. As the shaken hill begins to settle, his thoughts search for some explanation. *First the darkness, then this. What could it all mean?*

120

He looks up at Jesus, whose arms are raised, whose head is bowed. And the lifeless body seems to him to be an incarnate prayer. Slowly, a line at a time, the centurion reads the battered prose of this most sacred prayer. He sees

Arms reaching skyward at diagonals.
A spike through each wrist.
Lines of blood veining toward Jesus' chest.
A face mottled with fisted abuse.
Eyes swollen shut.
A ribcage torn and welted.
Knees turned to one side.
A single spike through both feet.
A thinning trail of blood, darkened at the edges.

As the centurion finishes the last, dark line of this silent prayer, he brushes away tears. Wondering, hoping, praying that the forgiveness he ignored only hours before is still available. For he truly did not know what he was doing. Or to whom he was doing it.

Until now.

There is a break in the darkness, and a spill of sunlight splashes onto the hill. A handful of disheveled soldiers hurry to the centurion's side, their minds racing with questions. He turns his eyes from the cross to the frantic circle of eyes that surround him. And he gives his explanation:

"Surely he was the Son of God!"

In his three short years as a preacher Jesus spoke from many pulpits. He spoke from a synagogue and from the side of a mountain. From the temple and from the dinner table of a tax collector. From the hull of a boat and from the home of a leper.

The cross would be his last pulpit. The crucifixion, his last sermon.

It was both the longest and the shortest he ever preached. Six hours of silence punctuated by a few sentences.

During those six hours, the centurion watched the way Jesus suffered and the way heaven responded to his suffering. It was a sermon he would never forget.

In a few hours Passover would begin. Not wanting to offend the Jews by desecrating their holy day with dead men, the centurion gives orders for the legs of the thieves to be broken. Now that the prisoners can no longer pull themselves up for air, they will suffocate. Death will come quickly, and the bodies will be down before dark.

Before Jesus is taken down, another soldier takes the point of a spear and counts his ribs. Between the fifth and sixth rib he positions the point. With a short thrust he punctures Jesus' heart. A confluence of blood and water streams from the wound. Convinced he is dead, the soldier leaves his legs unbroken and goes on to the next prisoner.

Before sundown all the prisoners are dead and off their crosses. Soon people all over Jerusalem will be celebrating the solemn Passover ritual of remembrance. They will remember the Exodus. And they will remember the plagues that made it possible, those labor pains in the womb of Egypt that led to the birth of their nation.

Especially they will remember that final, climactic plague, when the angel of death came for the firstborn sons. They will remember how the lamb was slaughtered. How its blood was smeared on the doorposts. How the angel saw the sign and passed over their houses.

Today the lamb that was slaughtered was Jesus. And the doorposts where the blood was smeared was the cross. But when the angel of death came, it did not spare this firstborn son.

That was the arrangement.

His life was not passed over so that ours might be . . . so that the timbers of *his* cross might become *our* doorway to heaven.

PRAYER

eautiful Savior,

Thank you for the prophetic picture of your sufferings
that was foreshadowed through the life of your servant
David. Certainly those words were on your heart as you
hung on that God-forsaken cross. Give me a few undis-
tracted minutes with that picture, Lord, so I may stand
silently before you now the way that centurion did so many
years ago. And slowly, a line at a time, let my eyes, as his
eyes did, read the battered prose of this most sacred prayer.

My God, my God, why have you forsaken
me?
Why are you so far from saving me,
so far from the words of my groaning?
O my God, I cry out by day, but you do not
answer,
by night, and am not silent.

Yet you are enthroned as the Holy One;
you are the praise of Israel.
In you our fathers put their trust;
they trusted and you delivered them.
They cried to you and were saved;
in you they trusted and were not disappointed.

But I am a worm and not a man,
scorned by men and despised by the people.
All who see me mock me;
they hurl insults, shaking their heads:
"He trusts in the Lord;
let the Lord rescue him.

Let him deliver him,
 since he delights in him."

Yet you brought me out of the womb;
 you made me trust in you
 even at my mother's breast.
From birth I was cast upon you;
 from my mother's womb you have been my God.
Do not be far from me,
 for trouble is near
 and there is no one to help.

Many bulls surround me;
 strong bulls of Bashan encircle me.
Roaring lions tearing their prey
 open their mouths wide against me.
I am poured out like water,
 and all my bones are out of joint.
My heart has turned to wax;
 it has melted away within me.
My strength is dried up like a potsherd,
 and my tongue sticks to the roof of my mouth;
 you lay me in the dust of death.
Dogs have surrounded me;
 a band of evil men has encircled me,
 they have pierced my hands and my feet.
I can count all my bones;
 people stare and gloat over me.
They divide my garments among them
 and cast lots for my clothing.

But you, O Lord, be not far off;
 O my Strength, come quickly to help me.

Deliver my life from the sword,
    my precious life from the power of the dogs.
Rescue me from the mouth of the lions;
    save me from the horns of the wild oxen.

I will declare your name to my brothers;
    in the congregation I will praise you.
You who fear the Lord, praise him!
All you descendants of Jacob, honor him!
Revere him, all you descendants of Israel!
For he has not despised or disdained
    the suffering of the afflicted one;
    he has not hidden his face from him
    but has listened to his cry for help.

AN
INTENSE MOMENT
ON THE
EMMAUS ROAD

SCRIPTURE

ow that same day two of them were going to a village called Emmaus, about seven miles from Jerusalem. They were talking with each other about everything that had happened. As they talked and discussed these things with each other, Jesus himself came up and walked along with them; but they were kept from recognizing him.

He asked them, "What are you discussing together as you walk along?"

They stood still, their faces downcast. One of them, named Cleopas, asked him, "Are you only a visitor to Jerusalem and do not know the things that have happened there in these days?"

"What things?" he asked.

"About Jesus of Nazareth," they replied. "He was a prophet, powerful in word and deed before God and all the people. The chief priests and our rulers handed him over to be sentenced to death, and they crucified him; but we had hoped that he was the one who was going to redeem Israel. And what is more, it is the third day since all this took place. In addition, some of our women amazed us. They went to the tomb early this morning but didn't find his body. They came and told us that they had seen a vision of angels, who said he was alive. Then some of our companions went to the tomb and found it just as the women had said, but him they did not see."

He said to them, "How foolish you are, and how slow of heart to believe all that the prophets have spoken! Did not the Christ have to suffer these things and then enter his glory?" And beginning with Moses and all the Prophets, he explained to them what was said in all the Scriptures concerning himself.

As they approached the village to which they were going, Jesus acted as if he were going farther. But they urged him strongly, "Stay with us, for it is nearly evening; the day is almost over." So he went in to stay with them.

When he was at the table with them, he took bread, gave thanks, broke it and began to give it to them. Then their eyes were opened and they recognized him, and he disappeared from their sight. They asked each other, "Were not our hearts burning within us while he talked with us on the road and opened the Scriptures to us?"

Luke 24:13–32

MEDITATION

It is called Good Friday. But for these two followers of Jesus nothing about it was good. Everything good that day had died. And it seems to them it will be Friday for the rest of their lives.

For the rest of Jerusalem, though, it's Sunday. The Passover Sabbath is over, and life has returned to normal.

But for these two men the sounds of life returning to normal seemed a sacrilege. For them nothing could ever be normal again.

No Passover could come without memories of him who was led as a lamb to the slaughter. No sacrifice could be made without remembering the way he was sheared and cut up and stretched out on that God-forsaken cross.

Since these two were friends of the man on that cross, a lot of strangers wanted to ask them questions, find out exactly what happened, and exactly what the disciples were going to do now.

But the two were so disoriented from grief they didn't know anything vaguely, let alone exactly. And what they did know, they didn't want to talk about. Especially with strangers.

And since the city was a spilling silo of strangers, they wanted out. They decide the country would be a good place to go, where there is space to think, to talk, to sort things out.

And they have plenty to sort. They have left everything behind to follow Jesus. They have staked their future on his words—their hopes, their dreams, everything. Now he is gone. And somehow they will have to get along without him.

But where will they go?

For now, anywhere. As long as it is away.

Away from the rubble of lives that have fallen apart. Lives that seem impossible to rebuild. Futile to even try.

So they go to try to sort things out, to try to understand what went wrong and why, and to try to decide where to go next.

They could take any of several roads. The road north of Jerusalem leads to Ephraim, but that is too far. The road east leads to Jericho, but that is too dangerous. The road south leads to Bethlehem, but that is too glaring a reminder of all they were wanting to forget. And so they take the road west.

The road to Emmaus.

The road to Emmaus is the road we take after we've been to Golgotha. It's the road we take when the other roads we've taken turn out to be dead ends. It's the road out of town, the road to getting away from it all.

They leave Jerusalem because there is nothing there for them anymore. Nothing but memories of a might-have-been Messiah. And what the world did to him.

But though what the world did to him is over, the pain is not. There's the headache and the heartache and the hard lump in the throat. There's the doubt and the dead-end questions and the dark night of the soul.

These were their thorns. These were their nails. These were their crosses. And they carry all these with them on the road out of town.

They leave behind the rumors of his resurrection. They carry with them only the reality of his death. And their sadness.

The road they travel slopes slowly away from the city and then squirms around a convergence of hills. The simple composition of stone against sky is a welcomed change from the Corinthian complexity of Roman architecture that surrounded them in Jerusalem.

The expansive starkness of the terrain mirrors the landscape of their soul. The starkness makes room for solitude. And the solitude makes room for their thoughts, giving them a chance to uncurl from the fetal position they have been in the past few days.

As they walk, their thoughts stretch and breath into conversation. But the conversations are overcast with emotion. Tears come and go. So do their thoughts.

They think of the beautiful dream the Savior had—the coming of God's kingdom. When his will would be done on earth as it is in heaven. When nations would beat their swords into plowshares. When the wolf would lie down with the lamb. And there would be peace on earth. All the earth. And there would be goodwill among people. All people.

It was a beautiful dream. And a dream they shared.

But Friday shattered it.

"Who would have thought it would come to this?" Cleopas says. "Just a week ago. The crowds. The way they praised him. The joy in their voices. The tears streaming down their cheeks. The timing seemed so right, with Passover, and people from all over. I had so hoped . . ."

But the pieces of the dream are still sharp; his words fearful of going near them. So they hesitate at his lips, trembling.

"I had hoped too," says the other.

As they're consoling each other, a stranger comes, inviting himself not only into their company but into their conversation.

"What are you discussing together as you walk along?"

The question stops them. Their downcast eyes search the road for strength to answer.

"Are you only a visitor to Jerusalem and do not know the things that have happened there in these days?"

"What things?" Jesus asks.

And they tell him the whole sad story. "And we hoped he was the one . . . the one who would redeem Israel."

Since the time they first met Jesus, they hoped he was the king he claimed to be. And they waited for him to usher in the kingdom.

133

But then he died.

And they hoped again, based on his word, that in three days he would return.

And they waited again. Friday. Saturday. Sunday morning. Sunday noon. Sunday afternoon.

Then they lost hope. Another one of Friday's casualties.

And without hope they couldn't wait any longer. So they left.

But there were other words besides the ones spoken by Jesus. Words that would have helped them understand his words. Words they should have known and should have remembered and should have believed.

"How foolish you are, and how slow of heart to believe all that the prophets have spoken! Did not the Christ have to suffer these things and then enter his glory?"

Jesus does not chide them for not believing the testimony of the women or the testimony of the empty tomb. He chides them for not believing the testimony of Scripture.

Then book by book, beginning with Genesis, Jesus rekindles the fire in their lives that suffering has all but extinguished. Step by step, the wood begins to dry. Verse by verse, the sparks find places to live. And by the time they reach Emmaus, their hearts are burning.

The three of them stop at the outskirts of town. The sun has continued on ahead of them, leaving an etching on the horizon where there were once hills. Jesus starts to continue on too, but they beg him to stay. Which he does.

They find a place to stay, and they sit together and start to eat, when suddenly . . .

The stranger is the Savior!

As soon as they recognize him, though, he vanishes.

Though life had caved in on these two men, enough light came through the fallen debris and airborne dust to give them hope. They couldn't see everything. But they could see him. And that was enough.

Enough to give them the strength to dig their way out.

Enough to keep them from giving in to their sadness or giving up on their hopes.

Enough so they could go on living, go on believing, and go back to Jerusalem to pass around the hope to those there who so desperately needed it.

PRAYER

ear Lord Jesus,

Thank you that whatever road I take to get away from the pain in my past, that is the road where you meet me. Thank you that even as I am walking away, you are walking after me. Wanting to draw near. Offering your companionship. Hoping to clear up the confusion in my life.

Thank you for your Word that sheds so much light on whatever road I take. Without it, how would I have ever found my way? Or my way back?

Help me to be sensitive to the way you speak to me through that Word. And to be sensitive to the many other ways you speak, which are often unfamiliar ways, spoken in unfamiliar voices from unfamiliar faces.

Thank you for the searching conversations that can only take place on the Emmaus road. Please break into those conversations, Lord, especially when I'm walking away and wondering why hopes I believed would come true didn't. Why suffering I prayed would be relieved wasn't. Why questions I asked to be answered weren't.

Stay with me, Lord, especially in times when I am disheartened. Show yourself to me, even if it is only for a moment. For your presence means more to me than my understanding. And seeing you when life doesn't make sense is better than not seeing you when it does.

Just as I pray you would be with me in my suffering, I pray I would be with you in yours. Help me to be with you in your weakness in the wilderness, with you in your tears on the road to Jerusalem, with you in your agony in Gethsemane, with you in your tortures on the cross.

Help me to understand something of the depths of your pain that I may appreciate more fully the depths of your love.

Thank you for the good that has come from the suffering I have known so far in this life. It has helped me learn to feel, and for that I am thankful.

The pain I have experienced has made me more sensitive to the pain of others. Thank you for that, Lord. And the sorrow I have known has made me more sympathetic to the sorrow of others. Thank you for that too.

And thank you that in the hunger I have known in the wilderness and in the thorns and nails I have known in the world, I have learned to feel something of the pain you felt when you walked this earth . . . and something of the fellowship of your sufferings, an intimacy with you I would have never known apart from tears. . . .

"To this you were called,
because Christ suffered for you,
leaving you an example,
that you should follow in his steps."